RIGHTING CANADA'S
WRONGS

Italian Canadian Internment
in the Second World War

Pamela Hickman and Jean Smith Cavalluzzo

JAMES LORIMER & COMPANY LTD., PUBLISHERS
TORONTO

James Lorimer & Company Ltd., Publishers acknowledges the support of the Ontario Arts Council. We acknowledge the financial support of the Government of Canada through the Canada Book Fund for our publishing activities. We acknowledge the support of the Canada Council for the Arts, which last year invested $24.3 million in writing and publishing throughout Canada. We acknowledge the Government of Ontario through the Ontario Media Development Corporation's Ontario Book Initiative.

Library and Archives Canada Cataloguing in Publication

Hickman, Pamela
    Italian Canadian internment in the Second World War / Pamela
Hickman and Jean Smith Cavalluzzo.

(Righting Canada's wrongs; 2)
Includes bibliographical references and index.
Issued also in electronic format.
ISBN 978-1-4594-0095-5

    1. Italian Canadians--Evacuation and relocation, 1940-1945--Juvenile literature. 2. World War, 1939-1945--Italian Canadians--Juvenile literature. 3. World War, 1939-1945--Prisoners and prisons, Canadian--Juvenile literature. 4. Italian Canadians--History--20th century--Juvenile literature. I. Smith Cavalluzzo, Jean II. Title. III. Series: Righting Canada's wrongs; 2

D805.C3H52 2012   j940.53'1771

C2012-902727-8

James Lorimer & Company Ltd., Publishers
317 Adelaide Street West, Suite 1002
Toronto, ON, Canada M5V 1P9
www.lorimer.ca

Printed and bound in Canada.

Manufactured by Friesens Corporation in Altona, Manitoba, Canada in August 2012.
Job # 78580

This book is dedicated to the families who shared their stories with me and to the wives and children of internees who coped and suffered without their husbands and fathers.

—J.S.C.

For my children, Angela, Connie and Jenny who are each contributing to a better, tolerant and enlightened Canada.

—P.H.

Acknowledgements

The collection of images for this book was a big undertaking and I'd like to thank those who were of special assistance in this task. In particular, Jean Smith Cavalluzzo for her personal contributions, Keith Minchin, Ed Caissie of the New Brunswick Internment Camp Museum, Columbus Centre, Angela and Connie Hickman, Multicultural History Society of Ontario, Ontario Archives, Beaton Institute, Ron Caplan, the City of Toronto Archives, Pier 21 Archives, Windsor's Community Museum, Ariella Hostetter and the Italian Canadian Community Centre of the National Capital Region, Library and Archives Canada, and all of the individuals and families who contributed personal documents and photos for this book.

— P.H.

I am indebted to my friend Donna McMillan for reading and editing my manuscript. I also thank Rita Bruno for sharing her taped video interviews with me and Luigi Pennacchio for reading and commenting on my first manuscript. For helping me to understand the perennial question of "How governments should respect civil liberties, while protecting our national security", I am forever thankful to my husband, Paul Cavalluzzo. I further thank Pal Di Iulio, Dr. Gabriele Scardellato, Kenneth Bagnell, Joseph Colangelo, and Angelo Prinicipe for their insight and analysis of the complexities of the Italian Canadian internment.

*   I thank my children, John-Paul and Angela Cavalluzzo, who help make the world a better place.*

*   I was privileged to interview many fine individuals and families who shared their stories, mementos, and pictures with me. I am particularly grateful to the following individuals without whom this book would not be possible: Paul Iannuzzi, Monique and Arnold Iannuzzi, Benny Ferri, Nicholas Zaffiro, Enrica Pataracchia Violin, Frank Martinello, Jenny Tamburro McQuillan, Dr. Rocco Tamburro, Eleanor Mogavero Loreti, George Iantorno, Rose Papalia Santagato, Frank Jannetta, Leonard D'Amico, Anita Lorenzetti McBride, and Dr. Michael Scandiffio.*

*   The following agencies and organizations provided me with archival material: Frank Iacobucci Centre for Italian Studies, City of Toronto Archives, National Archives of Canada, Archives of Ontario, Toronto Fire Department, Multicultural Historical Society of Ontario, Villa Charities and Columbus Centre of Toronto, and I thank them.*

—J.S.C.

Contents

WATCH THE VIDEO

Look for this symbol throughout the book for links to video clips available on the website *Italian Canadians as Enemy Aliens: Memories of World War II*, at www.italiancanadianww2.ca

Yukon

Northwest
Territory

Nunavut

British
Columbia

Alberta

Canada

Manitoba

Saskatchewan

Quebec

Newfoundland
& Labrador

Ontario

Newfoundland
& Labrador

Kamloops

Trail

Cape
Breton Island

Camp
Kananaskis

P.E.I

Sydney

Calgary

New
Brunswick

Nordegg

Winnipeg

Nova Scotia

Halifax

Thunder Bay
(formerly Fort William
and Port Arthur)

Sudbury

Montreal

Camp Ripples,
Minto

Camp Petawawa

Toronto

Kingston

Hamilton

Windsor

Brantford

Friuli-Venezia Gulia Region

Venice

Genoa

Italy

Molise Region

Naples

Grimaldi

Calabria Region

Amato

Sicily

Introduction

Italian immigration to Canada began in earnest in the late 1800s and early 1900s. Many agricultural workers and craftsmen left the hardship and poverty of southern Italy and arrived in Canada to find work and a better future for themselves and their families. Most of the arrivals were young single men or older men who left their families behind in Italy while they tried to establish themselves in Canada. Sometimes it was many years before wives and children were able to join their husbands and fathers. Their isolation in Canada was difficult for these early immigrants since family was a very important part of their culture. Men often sent word back to their home villages, encouraging other men to join them abroad. When families joined them, they usually settled for good in their new country.

Italian immigrants worked hard in labour-intensive jobs, especially building the Trans-Canada railway, constructing roads and sewers in the cities, and working in mines, forestry, and on farms. Although the Canadian government and its majority of citizens of British heritage often did not welcome immigrants from Italy, these pioneers persevered and found success. In some of the major Canadian cities they established Little Italies, communities where they lived with people who shared their heritage, culture, and language. Part of their social lives included membership in a variety of clubs for families, youth, and women, as well as after-work clubs. Some of these organizations were established by the Italian consuls who represented the Italian government in Canada.

When Benito Mussolini's Fascist government took power in the 1920s in Italy, his reforms generated praise from Italians around the world, as well as from

leaders of many countries, including Canada. In the mid to late 1930s, however, Fascist policies began to worry European and North American governments. Italy invaded the African country of Ethiopia in 1935, an action which was severely criticized by most democratic governments. At that point the Canadian government began to make a list of active supporters of the Italian Fascist government throughout Canada, but particularly among Italian communities. They were assisted by some Italian Canadians who became informants for the government.

When Italy joined in the Second World War on Nazi Germany's side on June 10, 1940, Canada immediately declared war on Italy. Instantly the Italian Canadian community was targeted by the RCMP and approximately six hundred people were arrested and imprisoned without charges. They were held in internment camps in British Columbia, Ontario, and New Brunswick for periods that ranged from months to years. No internees were ever charged or convicted of any crimes. Not only was their internment unjust and humiliating, but it also separated families at a time of great need. The wives and children of internees suffered great hardship as their main breadwinners were gone and there was often very little money available to them. Governments denied Italian-Canadian families social assistance. Many children had to leave school to work, to help support their families. Even men and women who were not interned often lost their jobs because they were of Italian descent.

Life after internment was not always easy, either. Some men were unable to get their jobs back and some were prevented from returning to their communities, so their families had to move.

In the late 1940s, after the war, the Canadian government opened up immigration to Italians once again. A new wave of Italian immigrants came by the thousands, revitalizing Italian communities. There are many Little Italies in larger Canadian cities today that represent a vibrant and proud Italian-Canadian population. Italian Canadians maintained their culture while achieving great success within mainstream Canada.

Following the Canadian government's official apology to Japanese Canadians for their unjust internment during the Second World War, the National Congress of Italian Canadians also sought an apology and redress. In 1990, Prime Minister Brian Mulroney apologized for the internment of Italian Canadians and admitted that it was unacceptable and wrong.

In this book you will meet many members of the Italian-Canadian community, some of whom were teens or children at the time when Canada and Italy were at war. In their own words, they tell what it was like to see their fathers arrested and how their lives changed while the heads of the families were interned. Others describe the sudden hostility

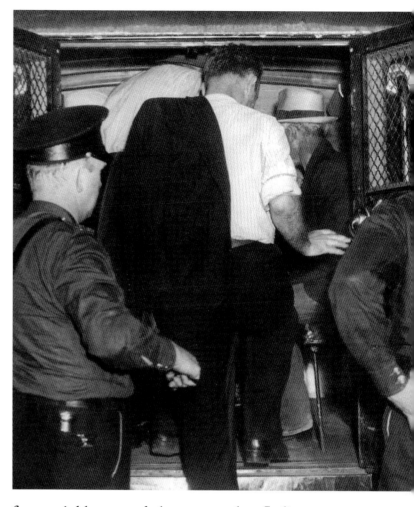

from neighbours and classmates when Italians were declared enemy aliens. They suffered discrimination, poverty, humiliation, and, in some cases, lack of basic education. Nick Zaffiro, Paul Iannuzzi, Dan Iannuzzi Jr., Frank Martinello, Rose Papalia Santagato, Enrica Pataracchia Violin, Jenny Tamburro McQuillan, Dr. Rocco Tamburro, Eleanor Mogavero Loreti, Ninetta Frenza, George Iantorno, Sal Pantalone, Kay Costantini, Italo Tiezzi, John Edward De Toro, and Londo Scattolon share their stories about being young Italian Canadians during a very troubled time in the country's history. In addition, the stories of internees Benny Ferri, James Franceschini, Frank Zaffiro, Dan Iannuzzi Sr., Domenic Nardocchio, and others illustrate how their lives were forever changed because of their internment.

Seeking a Better Life

In 1497, Giovanni Caboto (better known as the explorer John Cabot) was the first Italian to come to Canada, but it wasn't until the late 1800s that Italian immigrants began to arrive in larger groups.

Italy was a newly united country after 1870 and it wanted to become a powerful European nation. Most of its people lived in rural areas and worked in agriculture or were small-scale craftsmen. Times were hard, crops were poor, and many farmers couldn't make a living or feed their families from their small parcels of land.

The new Italian government wanted to develop industry in the northern part of the country. To fund their plans, they raised the taxes of the already poor rural population. Large numbers of desperate Italians began to leave their country, searching for a place where they could work and earn enough money to live a decent life.

No hope
In the south of Italy, much of the land was owned by wealthy people. Peasant labourers, such as the ones shown above, worked it for little pay. They had no hope of saving enough money to buy their own land.

Forced to leave
In this picture, a poor farmer ploughs his land using oxen. Even peasants who owned land often could not feed their families from it. They were forced to leave home for months at a time to find work in other industries and sometimes even in neighbouring countries.

Poverty
In southern Italian cities such as Naples, pictured above, many children grew up in poverty because their parents couldn't find enough work to pay for food and the increasing taxes that were piled on them.

Slaves in the sulphur mines
In Sicily, the large island off the southern tip of Italy, sulphur mines were a last resort for poor labourers who could not support their families and were desperate. The working conditions were terrible and the pay was bad. Even worse was the practice of selling their sons into a form of slavery to the mines. Poverty-stricken parents received a small payment in the form of a loan from the mining company. They needed this money to feed their starving families. In return, their young sons, seen here in this painting, had to work at back-breaking labour in the mines to pay off their parents' debts.

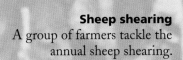

Sheep shearing
A group of farmers tackle the annual sheep shearing.

Women worked too
Many women worked in the fields to help their families.

Shepherd
Peasants, such as this shepherd, earned a meagre living by raising sheep for food and wool.

Large families
Most Italian immigrants came from rural villages and were part of large families. Usually, the men left behind their families while they searched for a new and better home away from Italy.

Unemployed
This group of men is sitting around a village square in Italy around 1890, waiting for work. If someone needed to hire help, he would come to the square and choose some men for the day. Lack of work was a big reason why many Italians left their homes for a new start in life.

Village life
Life in a village in nineteenth-century Italy was very basic. These Italian women are doing laundry by hand outdoors.

Factory work
Some people found jobs in factories in the larger Italian cities. These men are working in a munitions factory making ammunition.

Women factory workers
This photo shows women working in a munitions factory in early 1900s Italy.

Out-competed
As the industrialization of the north progressed, traditional craftsmen who worked in popular trades, such as ceramics, were out-competed by newer and larger factories. This picture shows a traditional ceramics mill in Italy.

City work
This woman is working in a factory in an Italian city in the early 1900s. Many women had to leave their children with family members while they went to work in city factories to help support their families.

"About 16 million Italians left Italy in the late 1800s and early 1900s to seek better lives."

Funding for Factories
In the late 1800s and early 1900s, the Italian government raised taxes across the country to help pay for the new industrial development in the country's north.

Farewells
About 16 million Italians left Italy in the late 1800s and early 1900s to seek better lives. Many headed to the agricultural areas of South America or the large construction projects, including roads, sewers, and railways, of North America. A small portion of these emigrants ended up in Canada.

The Immigrants

Early Italian immigrants to Canada were mainly single young men and teens or older men who left their families in Italy while they established themselves overseas. Most came from small rural towns and villages with populations of less than 10,000. They were skilled in a wide variety of trades, including agriculture, metalwork, stonework, woodwork, textiles, and industrial work. Some immigrants came to Canada planning to stay only a few years and then go back home with their savings. Others left Italy for good. Some Italians came directly to Canada, but many went to the United States first and then entered Canada later to find work.

Young family
Although most men emigrated alone, some brought their families with them. Here, a young Italian immigrant family poses in the late 1800s.

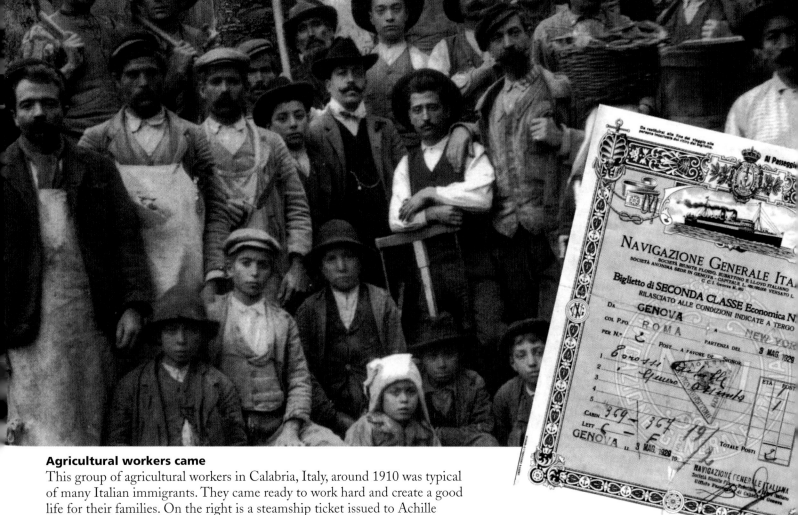

Agricultural workers came
This group of agricultural workers in Calabria, Italy, around 1910 was typical of many Italian immigrants. They came ready to work hard and create a good life for their families. On the right is a steamship ticket issued to Achille Torossi in 1929.

Young and adventurous

Giovan Battista Mottola was just twenty-four years old when this passport was issued in 1924. He was about to begin his adventure in Canada.

Families reunited

If a man with a family got a steady job in Canada, he would send for his wife and children. Annette Morello was six months old when her father left for Canada. She was seven when she and her mother joined him in Winnipeg. "When we came in 1933 and met him in the railway station, he said to me, 'Well, who is this cute little girl?' I said, 'Can't you tell that it's me?! Your daughter?'" Annette is pictured on the left in the 1940s with her sister, Teresa, and brother, Murray.

Chain migration

When men from the same Italian village were successful in their move to Canada, they would send word back home and encourage others to follow them. This flow of immigrants from one area was called chain migration. Many of these school children in Grimaldi, Italy, ended up in Canada because their fathers followed neighbours overseas.

The Immigrants   15

"They came ready to work hard and create a good life for their families."

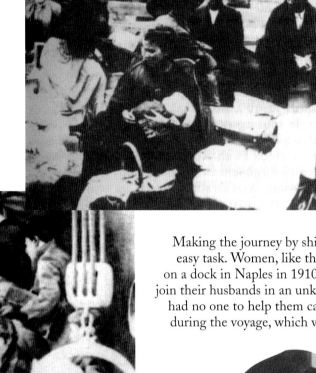

A tough trip
Making the journey by ship to Canada was no easy task. Women, like the ones pictured here on a dock in Naples in 1910, left their homes to join their husbands in an unknown country. They had no one to help them care for their children during the voyage, which was often very rough and dangerous.

▶️ **WATCH THE VIDEO**

Leaving home
James Franceschini was fifteen years old when he left his father and boarded a ship to a new life. He arrived in New York City and took a train to Toronto, where he was promised a job. He was handed a pick and a shovel — and that was the beginning of his multi-million dollar career.

Watch James McCreath discuss his grandfather James Franceschini's experiences coming to Canada at tinyurl.com/internment3

Gone for good
When Virginia Sherbo and her mother left Amato, Italy, to join her father in Winnipeg, her grandmother cried, "I'll never see you again." Most families that reunited in Canada didn't go back to Italy. When Virginia arrived in Winnipeg she met her father, a man she didn't know or recognize since he had emigrated when she was very young. Virginia is pictured here with her husband, August Cosentino, in Winnipeg in 1945.

Follow the leader
This Italian woman was likely following her husband to Canada in the 1920s. Once there, she would encourage other family members to join them. When extended families were together in Canada, they usually became permanent residents.

From ship to train
After making the long and difficult voyage across the ocean, many Italian immigrants had to make their way inland to find a place to settle. These newly arrived immigrants, mainly men, are at the train station in Winnipeg in 1927.

Why Choose Canada?

When Italian immigrants began to arrive, Canada was a new country with plenty of land waiting to be settled. The building of railways across the country was a huge source of work for thousands of immigrants, including many young Italian men. The cities, too, were under construction and they needed labourers to build roads, sewers, and other infrastructure.

When poor or dissatisfied Italians heard about their countrymen who had found a new life in Canada, they were often eager to follow. Some of the few Italian women who came to Canada in the early years ran boarding houses in the cities, such as Toronto and Hamilton, that welcomed new immigrants. Soon, small Italian communities formed far from their homeland.

Looking for workers
This poster was designed to attract men to Canada to work on the Canadian Pacific Railway (CPR).

CANADA

THE BUREAU OF CANADIAN INFORMATIO
DEPT. OF COLONIZATION & DEVELOPMEN
CANADIAN PACIFIC RAILWA
MONTREAL — LONDON — NEW YORK — CHICA

People needed

Canada's first prime minister, Sir John A. MacDonald, was in a hurry to settle the Prairies and build a transcontinental railway to connect the East to the West. His promise of the railway encouraged British Columbia to join Canada in 1871. Now the contractors needed the labour to build it. Canada campaigned hard in Britain and Europe to find settlers for the Prairies and labourers for the railway. This huge demand for labour encouraged private employment agents to set up business and build their fortunes on the backs of poor immigrants.

Lured to Canada

A little girl stands in front of her father's steamship agency on Agnes Street in Toronto around 1910. The agents got a commission on the tickets they sold and collected fees from emigrants for information regarding employment. A report of the deputy minister of labour in *The Labour Gazette* from June 1906 stated, "I am inclined to think that many of them should properly be considered as fraudulent employment agencies." Hamburg Amerika Lines had at least five steamers dedicated exclusively to the Italian trade.

Full of hope

Many Italian immigrants were full of hope when they went through the door of this provincial immigration and colonization office in Winnipeg in the early 1900s.

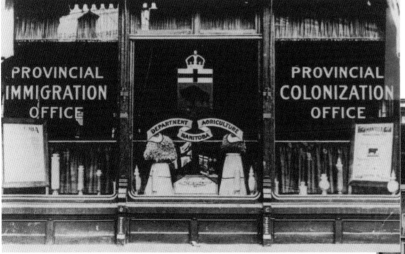

Promises of work

Employment agencies, often in association with Canadian railway and shipping companies, lured thousands of Italian labourers to Montreal and Toronto with promises of jobs. Pictured here is D'Angelo's labour exchange in Toronto in 1915.

Help for new immigrants

Charities, such as the Italian Immigrant Aid Society founded in Montreal in 1902, helped thousands of immigrants who found themselves in Canada without work, families, or English-speaking skills.

Many single men ended up in crowded boarding houses, searching for work and depending on handouts for survival. The Italian Mutual Benevolent Society, seen here hosting a picnic in 1931, was another group that helped new immigrants survive in troubled times.

In Windsor, Ontario, a group of Italian men banded together in 1924 to establish a club to help new immigrants adjust to Canada but keep their Italian culture. Eventually they added a Mutual Benefit Society to provide financial help to those who were unable to work. The club was later renamed the Giovanni Caboto Club, and it still exists today.

King of the labourers

Antonio Cordasco, pictured here, worked with industries, such as railways, as a padrone in turn-of-the-century Montreal. He provided them with the labour they needed, as well as food and other provisions. The companies paid Cordasco good money for his services. He attracted thousands of Italian labourers to Canada with promises of full-time jobs. Each one paid Cordasco a fee for his services, often the only money they had. So Cordasco collected money from both ends of the deals. He crowned himself "King of the Labourers." Frequently, he brought over far more men than he had work for and they ended up unemployed and badly-off in Montreal. In addition, with a huge pool of labour available, industries were able to reduce wages because men were desperate for work.

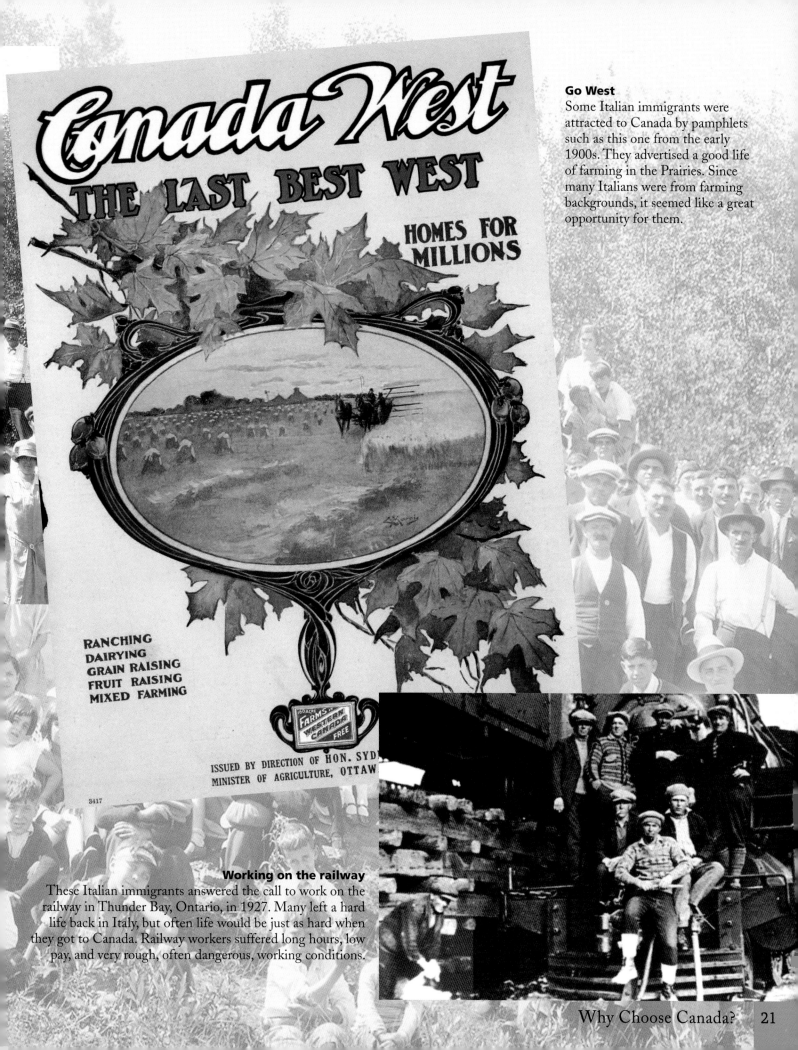

Canada West

THE LAST BEST WEST

HOMES FOR MILLIONS

RANCHING
DAIRYING
GRAIN RAISING
FRUIT RAISING
MIXED FARMING

160 ACRE FARMS IN WESTERN CANADA FREE

ISSUED BY DIRECTION OF HON. SYD
MINISTER OF AGRICULTURE, OTTAW

3417

Go West
Some Italian immigrants were attracted to Canada by pamphlets such as this one from the early 1900s. They advertised a good life of farming in the Prairies. Since many Italians were from farming backgrounds, it seemed like a great opportunity for them.

Working on the railway
These Italian immigrants answered the call to work on the railway in Thunder Bay, Ontario, in 1927. Many left a hard life back in Italy, but often life would be just as hard when they got to Canada. Railway workers suffered long hours, low pay, and very rough, often dangerous, working conditions.

Canada in the Early Twentieth Century

Canada was a very British society in the early twentieth century. Loyalty to the King of England was expressed every day by schoolchildren as they started their morning by singing "God Save the King" while gazing at the Union Jack, the flag of the British Commonwealth. When Britain went to war, Canada did too. Immigration favoured British, American, and northern European people. The white majority clearly preferred English-speaking, white, like-minded people with a culture similar to their own.

"I hope every City and District will win my flag"
H.R.H. Prince of Wales

Let us win the
PRINCE OF WALES' FLAG
VICTORY LOAN 1919

W.P. 9.

Canadian bobbies
Police officers, like the one pictured here in Toronto in 1907, wore British-style "bobby" uniforms.

Inspired by a prince
This Victory Loan war poster from 1919 shows the Prince of Wales as an inspiration to loyal Canadians. The campaign was a fundraising competition for Canadians after the First World War, to help the government recover from the great cost of the war.

Celebrating the Queen
Toronto's city streets were decorated for Queen Victoria's Diamond Jubilee in 1897. Notice the patriotic flags hanging from the buildings and a large image of Queen Victoria on the back of a streetcar.

The CNE
This program for the Canadian National Exhibition (the CNE) in Toronto in 1927 shows a large Union Jack. This was Canada's flag at the time because of its strong ties with Britain and the rest of the Commonwealth.

FFICIAL SOUVENIR
ALOG & PROGRAM
ONFEDERATION YEAR

QUEBEC PRINCE EDWARD ISLAND SASKATCHEWAN ALBERTA
MANITOBA ONTARIO NOVA SCOTIA BRITISH COLUMBIA

CANADIAN NATIONAL
1879—EXHIBITION—1927

AUG.
27
INCLUSIVE
CANADIAN NATIONAL
EXHIBITION
TORONTO
1927
SEPT.
10
INCLUSIVE

RECEPTION
TENDERED BY THE CITIZENS OF HALIFAX
TO
MEMBERS OF THE
Second Canadian Contingent
Artillery and Mounted Rifles
PRIOR TO THEIR DEPARTURE FOR SOUTH AFRICA
AT THE
NEW ARMOURY, HALIFAX,
Friday, Jan. 19th, 1900.

Fighting for the Empire
Canada joined the British Empire's fight in South Africa from 1899 to 1902. This is a program for a reception in Halifax, Nova Scotia, for troops leaving for the Boer War in 1900.

Men at Work

Canada's cities were growing as Canadians moved away from rural areas and more immigrants arrived. By 1930, there were about 100,000 Italians in Canada. In the cities, the men were mainly construction workers; craftsmen such as painters, plasterers, and stonemasons; small merchants; and storekeepers. They helped build roads, sewers, streetcar lines, and other major projects. Other Italian immigrants worked in farming in southern Ontario, the Prairies, or in British Columbia's orchards. Miners arrived from southern Italy and found work in western Canada, in northern Ontario, and in Cape Breton, Nova Scotia. The steel industry in Hamilton, Ontario employed many Italian Canadian workers.

Miners in the Maritimes
Cape Breton coal miners, many of whom were Italian, are seen here entering the pit in railcars, around 1930.

Hired for their class

Dofasco, a large steel company in Hamilton, was owned by C. W. Sherman. He encouraged the hiring of Italian workers, stating, "The reason we employ these men is because the work is of such a hot and laborious character that an English-speaking man will not do it . . . This class of labour has gradually changed from the hands of the Irishmen to the Slavs, and is now done entirely by the Italians."

Railway navvies

Railway construction was a big draw for many Italian labourers. Here, a group of Venetian navvies works on the CNR line in Kamloops, British Columbia, in 1911. "Navvies" was a term used for labourers who worked on construction or excavation projects such as railways and canals.

Farming

Some immigrants became farm labourers. These men worked in Ontario in 1900. Others were able to buy land and develop vineyards, vegetable farms, and orchards of their own.

Roadwork

Road construction was a big employer of immigrant labour. These men are laying cobblestone in Toronto in 1903. The disappointment felt by some Italians who came to Canada looking for the land of plenty that had been promised to them was expressed by the familiar quotation: "The streets were not paved with gold. The streets were not paved. We were expected to pave the streets."

Working underground

Sewer construction in Toronto in 1912. Note the lack of any safety equipment or protection from cave-ins.

Unsafe working conditions

These Italian labourers were building the storm overflow sewers in Toronto. They often worked without safety equipment or proper ventilation. In the early 1900s there was no minimum wage, no unemployment insurance, and no paid holidays for the workers. Wages on construction sites ranged from fifteen to twenty cents an hour.

Brick making

Skilled craftsmen often found jobs in the cities. These Friulian brick makers worked at the John Price plant of the Toronto Brick Company in the city's East End in 1936.

Shoemakers

Shoemaking was a skill that many Italians brought with them when they immigrated to Canada. Here, Montreal shoemaker Robert Amadori works in his shop.

"The streets were not paved with gold. The streets were not paved. We were expected to pave the streets."

Men at Work

Fruit sellers
Immigrants from Sicily, Rosario Sanfilipo and Salvatore Scaletta, pictured here in 1929, were fruit sellers in Winnipeg.

"By 1930 there were about 100,000 Italians in Canada."

Small-business owners
The Badalis were among the earliest Italian immigrants to Winnipeg. The Badali brothers are pictured here inside their Olympia Café in 1913.

Criminals and crime fighters

Organized crime was a growing concern in Ontario and Quebec in the pre-war years. Several Italian immigrants, such as Rocco Perri, Tony Papalia, and Domenico Longo, were known to run bootlegging, drug smuggling, and other illegal activities. Frank Zaneth (originally named Zanetti before he anglicized his name) was an Italian-Canadian RCMP officer assigned to investigate mobsters in Hamilton. He dedicated himself to convicting Rocco Perri, one of the leading rum smugglers and mobsters, but he never did.

Mining in Alberta
Italian immigrants working in a coal mine in Nordegg, Alberta, in the 1940s.

Armed forces

From 1914 to 1918, men of Italian descent found work in the Canadian Armed Forces, as did many young Canadians. These volunteers in the First World War are standing behind Mayor Tommy Church in Toronto, 1915.

Volunteers

Italian immigrant reservists, seen here in downtown Toronto, are marching off to war in 1915. This was a difficult time for many immigrants as the country was still recovering from the pre-war depression. It took a couple years before the war boom caught up with the high unemployment. Immigrants were often the ones that suffered most in these years.

Women at Work

Although the majority of early Italian immigrants were men, some wives travelled with their husbands. These women often ran the boarding houses where many Italian men lived while trying to establish themselves, find work, and earn enough money to marry or bring over families that they had left behind in Italy. As time went on, wives and children joined their husbands and fathers in Canada. Women were often fully occupied raising large families and trying to feed them on their husbands' meagre wages. Some women also worked outside of the home. Most often they were employed in offices, stores, and factories. As families became more successful and financially stable, many Italian-Canadian women took on volunteer work in the community, often related to Italian social clubs.

Working in the garment industry
Some Italian women found work in factories. These women worked in the garment industry in Toronto in 1908. Women working ten hours a day earned as little as four to seven dollars a week.

A family business
Barbara Pucci, pictured here in 1918 with her husband Ernesto, worked in the family business. The couple owned the Pucci Brothers Fruit and Confectionary in Winnipeg.

"Women working ten hours a day earned as little as four to seven dollars a week."

Extra work

When Rose Papalia Santagato's family came to Canada from Italy, her father worked at Union Station in Toronto. In order to help the family make ends meet, her mother took in boarders. She fed them and washed their clothes and sheets. Mrs. Papalia also had eight children to care for. The family is pictured here in 1933. Front row: Mrs. Papalia, Rose, Mr. Papalia; second row: sisters Kay and Betty; back row: Rose's five brothers.

Italian Red Cross volunteers

During the First World War, many Italian Canadians joined up to fight with the Allies or became reservists. Women volunteered, too. Here, women of the Italian Red Cross Society are pictured alongside a group of Italian-Canadian reservists in Toronto in 1915.

Community newspaper

Some women used their office skills to work on community newspapers. These women were the founders of *St. Anthony's Bulletin* in Toronto in 1931.

Italian Club Plans Royal Visit Dance

Social planning in the community

Socializing was a big part of Italian-Canadian family life. These women were members of the Italian Ladies' Independent Political Club in Windsor, Ontario. They were planning a dance in honour of the visit of King George VI and Queen Elizabeth in 1939. From left to right are Mrs. Orlando Bocchini, Bertha Noesella, and Derna Serafini.

Achievers in the Italian-Canadian Community

Many Italian immigrants worked very hard at difficult jobs when they came to Canada. They stuck with it and saved enough money to start their own businesses. Most began a business with the skills that they had brought with them from Italy. Half the fruit and vegetable shops in Toronto were owned by Sicilians. Whether it was a market garden, a brick or stoneworks, a restaurant, or a construction company, many Italian-Canadian business people prospered. Italian-Canadian communities grew up within many large Canadian cities and it was in these Little Italies that most of the new businesses were established.

Success
As Italian Canadians became financially successful, they often became socially successful as well, and integrated into Canadian society.

First photography studio
Emilio Galardo, pictured here with his family in 1932, established the first commercial photography studio in Sudbury, Ontario.

The shoe business
This Italian-owned shoe shine and repair shop offered a popular service in Calgary, Alberta, in 1929. Many shoemakers from Italy set up shops in cities and towns across Canada.

Popcorn!
Some businesses were quite small. This man was a popcorn vendor in Toronto in 1922.

Achievers in the Italian-Canadian Community   33

Tile and terrazzo

Baldo Camilotto is shown here in 1923 with one of the first Colautti Bros. trucks used in their tile and terrazzo contracting company in Windsor, Ontario. Many Italian immigrants were highly skilled at working with tile, brick, and stone.

Auto industry

The auto industry based in Windsor attracted many immigrants to work in the factories. Some also started their own related businesses in the community. Mario Bernachi founded the Windsor Body & Fender Company.

Italian goods for Italian immigrants

Italian Canadians shopped in this Italian general store in Ontario. They could speak their native language and buy familiar foods that weren't available in other Canadian shops.

Pre-war professional
Neldo (Ned) Lorenzetti was the first Canadian-born, Italian-speaking lawyer to practise in Toronto. He was active in the Italian community and president of the Canadian-Italian Businessmen's Association in Toronto.

Family business
James and Rosina Forte established their fruit market in Brantford, Ontario, in 1919. Since then it has passed down through the family and is now run by the third generation of Fortes.

"Thousands of Italian immigrants worked in construction when they came to Canada, especially in the cities."

▶ WATCH THE VIDEO

Construction company
Thousands of Italian immigrants worked in construction when they came to Canada, especially in the cities. That's how James Franceschini started out when he arrived in 1905 as a fifteen-year-old boy on his own. Within seven years, he founded a construction company. These Italian Canadians are at work on the construction of the CPR's West Toronto Station at Dundas Street and Royce Avenue in May 1925. The contractor for the project was Franceschini's Dufferin Construction.

▶ Watch James McCreath discuss his grandfather James Franceschini's business career at tinyurl.com/internment3 (Link also appears on p. 16)

Achievers in the Italian-Canadian Community

Italian Neighbourhoods

In many large Canadian cities, including Toronto, Montreal, Hamilton, Windsor, and Winnipeg, large Italian neighbourhoods developed. In these neighbourhoods were the key institutions of Italian-Canadian life, such as churches, schools, shops, news media, social clubs, and restaurants. Many of these Little Italies still exist today.

Church social
A large group of Italian Canadians gathers outside St. Joseph's church in Fort William, Ontario, for a community festival in 1920. The church was not only a source of spiritual guidance, but also served as a meeting place for community members.

Centre of the community
Italian immigrants began arriving in Ottawa as early as 1840. In 1913, the community built the Saint Anthony of Padua church. After it was destroyed by fire in 1917, a new St. Anthony's, pictured here, was built through the efforts of volunteers and a supportive congregation. It is a focal point of Ottawa's Little Italy.

Separate schools

Many Italian immigrants sent their children to schools that were run in association with the Roman Catholic Church. Pictured here is Notre Dame de la Défense school in Montreal's Little Italy.

Nova Scotia community

A large immigrant community existed in Whitney Pier, Nova Scotia. A number of Italian immigrants worked in the coal mines there. Frank Martinello was in this grade one class at Villa Nova School in 1934. He is in the middle of the back row wearing a black turtleneck and white suspenders.

▶ Watch Frank Martinello describe his childhood at tinyurl.com/internment5

▶ WATCH THE VIDEO

Home away from home

Toronto's Little Italy, pictured here, was lined with Italian fruit and vegetable shops, restaurants, and other businesses where local people could share their culture and feel at home.

Italian Neighbourhoods   37

College Street, Toronto
This view of Little Italy in Toronto taken before the Second World War includes businesses and residential buildings.

Support for mothers
The Italian Mothercraft program, pictured here in Toronto in 1916, offered programs to help and support immigrant mothers.

"Strong communities help those in need."

Winnipeg
Winnipeg's Little Italy was mainly in the West End of the city in the 1920s.

Italian Culture

Italian immigrants brought their language, religion, food preferences, skills, music, and social activities with them when they came to Canada. In other words, they brought their culture to their new country. Most Italians were Roman Catholic, so new churches, and sometimes separate schools, were established in their neighbourhoods. Many social clubs started up so Italians could meet in their free time to enjoy their own music and games, and relax with people who spoke their own language and shared their roots.

Garlic
Garlic is a staple ingredient in Italian cooking. It was considered strange and "smelly" by Canadians unfamiliar with Italian food.

Traditional Italian cooking
Italian cuisine, so common in Canada today, was very strange to non-Italian Canadians. Many Italian immigrant families planted huge backyard gardens full of ingredients for their prized sauces and other homemade foods. Women spent long hours at harvest time preparing preserves to last through the winter. Here, Pieirina Gargarella and Josephine Ciccone are making tomato paste in their Toronto backyard in 1936.

Folk dancers
Traditional Italian folk dancers and singers are seen here at Assiniboine Park in Winnipeg in 1931.

Catholic society
Many Roman Catholic churches were founded and attended by Italian immigrants. This is the Church of the Madonna della Difesa (Our Lady of Defense Church) in Little Italy, Montreal.

Confirmation
Children were often raised in their parents' religion and attended church regularly. When they reached their teens, they were usually confirmed, a ceremony in which they took their own vows to become active and committed members of the church. Eleanor Mogavero Loreti is pictured in her confirmation dress with her nephew, William, in 1939.

Italian Culture

Madonna festival
The Madonna festival is a special annual religious celebration that honours the Madonna. It usually begins with a religious service and is followed by an outdoor procession in which a statue of the Madonna is carried through the streets. Festivities often continue all day and into the evening.

Weddings
Italian weddings tended to be large affairs with many family and friends, lots of homemade food and wine, and a great celebration.

Funerals
Dying far away from one's birthplace was difficult to accept for many immigrants. The Italian-Canadian community carried on the traditional rituals of their homeland when it came to funerals. Here, a large group gathers for the funeral service for a local Toronto businessman in 1922.

Two flags
A 1915 rally in support of the First World War displays both Italian and Ontario flags flying together.

Italian teens
Young Italians also got together to hang out and share their culture. This notice announced a dance at the Italian Girls Club in Winnipeg in 1924.

Sharing their culture
Italian immigrants were proud of their heritage but they were also ready to accept their new country's heritage. This photo shows a float that the Italian community in Winnipeg put together to share in the Dominion Day parade in 1927.

Targets of Racism

Immigrants from many countries arrived in Canada in a steady stream in the late 1800s and early 1900s. They came to a country where racist attitudes and conduct towards many groups was common and socially accepted. Anti-immigrant attitudes were often expressed, and discrimination practised against a wide range of groups. Early Italian immigrants experienced widespread racism. Racism was institutionalized in hiring practices and immigration policies. It was expressed in the behaviour of English- and French-Canadian neighbours, businesses, and communities.

Not wanted

Clifford Sifton was minister of the interior from 1896 to 1905 under Prime Minister Wilfrid Laurier. Sifton's job was to settle the Prairies and bring in labour. He focused his campaigns on Britain and northern Europe but not southern Europeans. Sifton stated: "No steps are to be taken to assist or encourage Italian immigration to Canada . . ." Despite this official hostility, Italian immigrants arrived, settling mainly in eastern Canada at first.

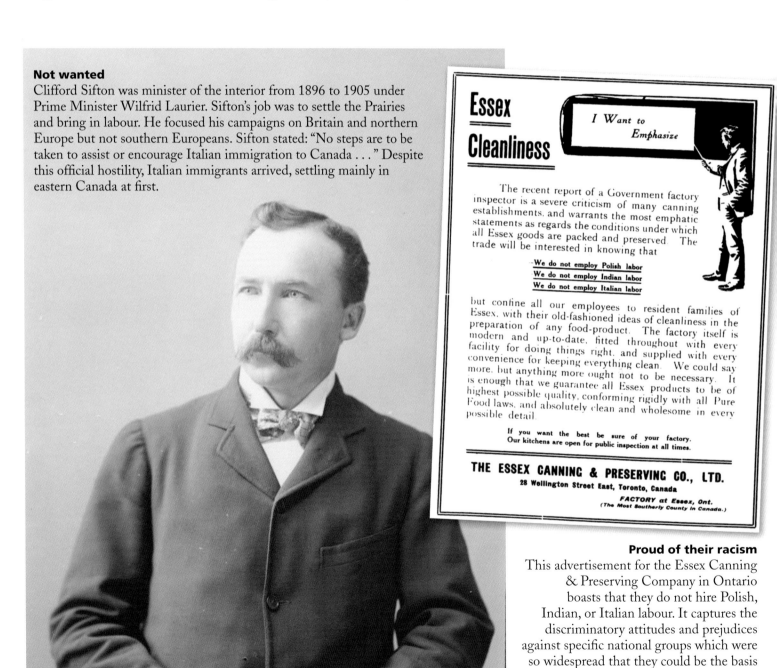

Proud of their racism

This advertisement for the Essex Canning & Preserving Company in Ontario boasts that they do not hire Polish, Indian, or Italian labour. It captures the discriminatory attitudes and prejudices against specific national groups which were so widespread that they could be the basis for an advertising campaign by a Canadian food company in the early 1900s.

"ALLAN" LINE ROYAL MAIL STEAMERS.

LIVERPOOL TO QUEBEC

The Last Best West

Canada
in the Twentieth Century
WESTERN CANADA
vast
Agricultural Resources
HOMES FOR MILLIONS

GRAIN RAISING. RANCHING. FARMS IN WESTERN CANADA FREE MIXED FARMING. DAIRYING.

ISSUED BY DIRECTION OF HON. FRANK OLIVER MINISTER OF THE INTERIOR OTTAWA, CANADA.

British values and culture

Frank Oliver followed Clifford Sifton as head of immigration from 1905 to 1911 and promoted western Canadian settlement. He believed that ethnic and cultural origins were more important than farming skills. He sought to reinforce British values and culture in Canada. In 1910 he championed a new immigration act that gave the government powers to control the numbers, ethnic origins, and occupations of immigrants.

Come if you're British

This Allan Line steamers advertisement is for trips from Liverpool in the United Kingdom to Quebec. Canadian immigration encouraged British immigrants but not Italians.

Few opportunities

The Toronto Police Department, seen here on parade in 1916, had few, if any, Italians on their force. Police, fire, and other public forces tended to hire people of British descent, which limited the opportunities for immigrants. There was only one Italian-Canadian officer on the Toronto force in the 1930s.

Name-calling

Geremino and Alfonsina Cordileone, shown here on their wedding day in Winnipeg in 1926, lived in a non-Italian neighbourhood during the 1930s and 1940s. Their neighbours did not always understand or appreciate their culture or customs. For example, the Cordileones made their own wine, a traditional activity in much of Europe but not in Canada. To avoid trouble, they had the grapes delivered in the night and then burned the wooden cases in their furnace. Neighbours called them racist names such as "wop" or "dago" or simply "those Italians."

Targets of Racism

Links to the Home Country

Italian immigrants were closely tied to their relatives who remained in Italy as well as the people in their home village. News of "the old country" came with new immigrants or by letters. Italian-Canadian newspapers also carried news from Italy. In this way, first-generation Italian immigrants in Canada felt connected to Italy while they adapted to being new Canadians. Their Italian roots were also reinforced daily through the Dopolavoro, which were after-work social clubs, and a variety of other social clubs for women, youth, and families.

Youth band
An Italian youth band (Gioventu del Littorio all'Estero) posed in front of the Casa d'Italia in Toronto. Arnaldo Miclet, the head teacher at the Casa d'Italia, is on the right.

Kids at camp
Many Italian-Canadian kids were sent to summer camps in Italy, courtesy of the Italian government. The camps helped Italian Canadians to maintain their connections and language. Here, a group of young women from Hamilton and elsewhere are shown at a resort in Genoa, Italy. They were exposed to pro-Fascist views and much praise for Mussolini and his government's achievements.

Rose Papalia Santagato goes to Italy

Rose Papalia remembers: "In 1936, I applied and was accepted to go with forty other students to Italy with the group 'Gioventu.' It was an exchange program where forty children would come here from Italy and children from Canada and the USA would visit Italy for five weeks. It was a trip of a lifetime. Imagine! The Italian government, I think, paid for most of the trip. I was lucky my parents let me go on the trip because I was only thirteen years old. We arrived in Genoa and visited Milan, Rome, and many other Italian cities. We were to meet the Italian president Benito Mussolini in Rome but he couldn't attend that day. Instead we met a general and other officials from the government. The highlight of the trip was being allowed to visit our 'hometowns' (where our parents were from). You can't imagine the impact and memories of that trip."

Montreal newspaper

L'Italia, a pro-Fascist paper published in Montreal, features a large picture of the Italian military on parade in Rome. The newspapers kept people informed about progress in Italy, and also served as a vehicle to spread pro-Fascist news and opinion throughout Italian immigrant communities.

News from home

Italian immigrants could stay in touch with news from Italy through newspapers such as the *L'Araldo del Canada*, an Italian-Canadian Fascist newspaper founded in 1906. This issue, dated 1930, shows a picture of the King of Italy, Vittorio Emanuele III, who was king throughout the rise and fall of Fascist Italy.

Fascism in Italy and Canadian Connections

Benito Mussolini led his National Fascist Party to seize power in Italy in 1922. He took complete political control of the country as a dictator and his paramilitary group of "Blackshirts" crushed all opposition, usually violently. Elections were abolished and Italy became a one-party state. Throughout the 1920s and 1930s, Italy's economy grew, industry increased, and living standards improved. At first, Mussolini's turnaround of Italy's fortunes was admired in many countries, including Canada.

Emigration from Italy was discouraged by the Fascists. They worked hard to encourage Italians around the world to support Fascism and take great pride in their Italian heritage. Italian government consulates were set up in countries where Italians had settled, including Canada. Case d'Italia were organized as social clubs requiring Fascist party membership. Many Italian-Canadian Fascist newspapers were published in Canada and they helped to generate pride and support among the immigrant community. Roman Catholic churches also promoted loyalty to Italy. There were an estimated 3,000 actively pro-Fascist Italian Canadians in Canada in the late 1930s.

Il Duce

Mussolini, also known as Il Duce, is standing front and centre on the podium. Nick Zaffiro was a child when his father was the secretary of the Fascio (Fascist party) in Hamilton. Later he asked his father why he was a Fascist. Frank Zaffiro told his son that when he left his hometown in 1923, there was no water in the house, the streets were dirt roads, there was no heat, and people didn't go to school. But when he went back in 1926, there was water and roads, school was mandatory, and crime was almost non-existent. That's what the dictatorship did. Nick explains, "The Mafia in those days would kill your sheep and oxen so you couldn't earn a living. If you complained to the police, they wouldn't enforce the law. That's the type of society they lived in. When Mussolini came in, there was law and order, education, social services, pensions, and medical care."

Fascist social clubs

This July 13, 1934, advertisement from *Il Bolletino Italo-Canadese*, a Toronto-based Fascist newspaper, commemorates Toronto's centennial. It was organized by Toronto's leading Fascist club, Fascio Principe Umberto, and the Italian War Veterans Association. Large Fascist groups existed pre-war, but many were mainly social in nature and members didn't consider the Fascist membership requirement as a commitment to support Mussolini's regime. Rose Papalia Santagato remembers going to the Casa d'Italia in Toronto when she was seventeen. "We were just social members. I do remember, though it's embarrassing now to think of, that we had to give the Fascist salute and sing the Fascist national anthem as part of the events. But it didn't mean anything to us politically. We weren't into the politics of Fascism, that's for sure."

L'Eco Italo-Canadese

Non dimenticarti sei ITALIANO

LA MODERAZIONE E' VENUTA DA ROMA

HITLER

Vancouver newspaper

L'Eco Italo-Canadese was a pro-Fascist newspaper in Vancouver. This 1938 front page features a large picture of Mussolini and a smaller one of Germany's Adolf Hitler. For many Italian Canadians, the attraction of Mussolini's government was not so much its anti-democratic politics but the rebirth of national pride and the strength of the economy.

Politics in the classroom

The Italian government created a worldwide school system that sent educational material to language schools overseas, including Canada. This book cover is from a reader that the Fascist Italian government provided in Ontario in the 1930s, titled *Il Primo Libro Del Fascista* (translation: *The First Fascist Reader*). From 1938 to 1939, over 600 children attended Italian language schools throughout Toronto. There was an uproar in the English-Canadian community when it was discovered that the lessons included pro-Fascist political material.

Italian invasion

When Italy attacked the African country of Ethiopia (then called Abyssinia) in 1935, there was great support from Italians around the world. About twenty-five young Italian-Canadian Fascists volunteered to fight for Italy in Ethiopia. Fundraising rallies in Italian communities collected money and valuables — even gold wedding rings — to support Italy's expansion. This aggression, however, made other countries cautious and suspicious. In Canada, public opinion turned against Fascism. Authorities began to watch the Fascist community with growing mistrust.

Fascism in Italy and Canadian Connections

Fascism and its Opponents in Canada

Within the Italian community there were left-wing as well as right-wing groups and individuals, each with their own newspapers to spread their ideas through the immigrant community. Before the Second World War started in 1939, there was much support for Mussolini's Fascist government among the Italian-Canadian community as well as among Canadians generally. Fascism attracted many non-Italian supporters across Canada. The most prominent Canadian Fascist party was led by Adrien Arcand, a French-Canadian journalist in Montreal. The Roman Catholic Church supported the Fascist leaders in part because they feared the perceived "Godless" threat of communism. In the wider Canadian community, fascism was often seen as preferable to the alternatives of socialism and communism.

In the 1930s the world economy was in turmoil. There were far too few jobs, especially for young people. Canadians were taking to the streets to protests conditions, and young people were looking for radical answers. Some Italian immigrants turned to the Protestant Church, the CCF (Co-operative Commonwealth Federation political party), and the Communist Party of Canada who had much different ideas about how to solve the world's obvious economic problems. Left-wing parties were strongly anti-Fascist as the world moved towards war.

Support for Mussolini and Fascism diminished when Italy adopted anti-Jewish legislation and staged its invasion of Ethiopia. Opponents criticized the Italian government's anti-democratic nature, its suppression of labour unions, and its absolute intolerance of opposition.

The Young Worker

This newspaper, published by the Young Communist League of Canada, is aimed at anti-Fascist Italian Canadians, as well as non-Italians. This October 1935 issue denounces Italy's invasion of Ethiopia and rallies its young readers to oppose the threat of fascism in Canada.

Anti-fascist press

La Voce degli Italo-Canadese was an all-inclusive anti-fascist newspaper. Many left-wing activist voices were represented, including communists, socialists, anarchists and Trotskyites; Christians, both Catholics and Protestants; and conservative and liberal anti-fascists. It was formed in 1938 in response to the anti-Semitic propaganda that was being published by the fascist press after Mussolini introduced anti-Jewish legislation in Italy. On the front page of this issue is a picture of the Italian Progressive Club parading at Queen's Park to celebrate May Day. The group was originally called the Italian Communist Club but they changed their name in 1939 when communist organizations were banned in Canada.

Arcand's loyal followers
Note the swastikas on the walls at this meeting of Arcand's fascist Parti National Social Chretien du Canada (PSNC) in Montreal in June 1938.

Canadian fascist leader

Adrien Arcand, pictured here, was a francophone Canadian based in Montreal and the leading Canadian fascist of the 1930s and 1940s. He was a vocal campaigner for the anti-democratic views of fascism, a fierce anti-Semite, and an admirer of Hitler, Mussolini, and other fascist leaders around the world. Arcand had a good relationship with the Italian-Canadian fascists. The Montreal-based Italian Fascists sometimes lent Arcand's followers their premises and even welcomed them to their meetings.

According to documents in the archives of the Canadian Jewish Congress in Montreal, Arcand participated in fascist events organized by the Montreal Italian community. In return, Arcand's PNSC received ongoing support from the Italian community in Montreal. In 1938, more than a thousand people, at least a third of whom were Italian Canadians, attended a meeting that Arcand held in Dante Hall in the Casa d'Italia. Italian Canadians were represented in the PNSC by Antonio Felli, one of the party's main organizers. Arcand also developed a bond with Dieni Gentile, one of the leaders of Montreal's Italian Fascist circles. Arcand drew the majority of his support from non-Italian francophone Canadians.

Accused

Arcand and other leading fascists in 1940 were arrested and put on trial. They were quickly accused and convicted of "plotting against the government" and sent off to internment camp. In this photo are Dr. Noel Decarie, Maurius Gatien, Maurice Scott, John Loriner, Joseph C. Farr, Arcand and his brother Henry, Leo Brunet, and G. R. Barck.

Facism and its Opponents in Canada

CHAPTER 4
CANADA AT WAR

Canada joined Britain in declaring war on Germany in 1939. At first Italy, who had fought alongside Britain in the First World War, stayed silent. Because of Italy's aggression against Ethiopia a few years earlier, and the fact that it had not joined the war against Germany, Italy was being watched by the Allies. In Canada, the RCMP had the Italian community under surveillance and developing lists of Fascist supporters. The RCMP also kept lists of Communist sympathizers, as they were considered an even greater threat to security.

The Canadian government rallied all Canadians to support the troops, work hard, and make sacrifices at home to ensure victory. Thousands of men and women joined the armed forces, including Italian Canadians.

Germany invaded France and drove British forces to withdraw from France back to Britain. The Germans looked almost unstoppable. Mussolini joined the fascist German government of the Nazi Party led by Adolf Hitler in an alliance against Britain. On June 10, 1940, Canada declared war on Italy. The news of Italy's alliance with Germany came as a terrible shock to many Italian Canadians. Overnight, their relationships with their friends, neighbours, fellow employees, and classmates changed for the worse.

Posters everywhere
During the war, Canada produced hundreds of posters like this one. Canadians were constantly encouraged to give money to support the war.

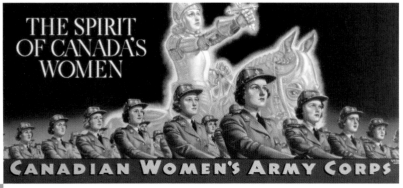

A new target
This Canadian Women's Army Corps poster targeted a new source of recruits — women.

Ready, aim, fire!
A young boy aims his baseball at Mussolini's face in a midway game at Toronto's Canadian National Exhibition in 1940. Fear and loathing of Fascism wasn't restricted to adults.

"News of Italy's alliance with Germany came as a terrible shock to many Italian Canadians."

Captured
SS *Capo Noli*, above, was an Italian ship caught sailing out of the St. Lawrence Seaway when Canada declared war on Italy on June 10, 1940. The sailors were captured and interned as prisoners of war (POWs).

Italian Canadians Join the War Effort

When Canada joined Britain and its allies to declare war on Germany in 1939, the Canadian population was asked for their support. Many Italian immigrants in Canada helped out through buying Victory Bonds and signing up to fight. After Italy joined up with Germany, many Italian organizations immediately pledged their allegiance to Canada and its allies. They wanted it to be clear that they did not support Italy in the war.

Fighting for his right to fight
Victor Pucci was born in Canada to Italian immigrants from Calabria. He served in the navy during the Second World War. One of his commanders refused to allow him to enter torpedo school because of his Italian heritage. Eventually a chief petty officer, who was also of Italian descent, got him the documents necessary to attend the school.

Italian Canadians signed up
There were no restrictions on people of Italian descent fighting for Canada during the war. Rose Papalia Santagato recalls, "When the war broke out in 1939, I had five brothers who all enlisted in the Canadian services. My family was very proud. Three of my brothers were needed in Canada but Tully and Joe went overseas."

Merry Christmas
Gus Cosentino, a young Italian-Canadian sailor, sent this Christmas card home in 1943.

Victory Gardens
The war effort campaign encouraged people to grow their own food, so there was more food to send overseas to the troops. Here, Augustine Di Tourneso plants his Victory Garden in Toronto in 1940.

Support and sacrifice
Many Italian-Canadian associations held fundraisers for the war effort. Others sent their family members off to war.

Kids helped too
School kids were encouraged to collect metal, paper, and other materials that could be recycled for the war effort. Here, children are collecting aluminum. Jenny Tamburro McQuillan was a child during the war. She remembers trying to be a "super collector." During one paper drive, she and her brother collected paper and filled their basement to the rafters. It took them days to deliver the papers to their school by wagon. Achieving status by collecting the most paper was important to them. "We were Canadian born and just trying to show that we too were Canadians."

Italian Canadians Join the War Effort

CHAPTER 5
ENEMY ALIENS

Italian Canadians Become Enemy Aliens

Immediately after Italy's declaration of war on June 10, 1940, Canada applied the *War Measures Act* to its Italian residents. Those over eighteen years of age (military age) and Italian citizens were declared enemy aliens, along with those who had become Canadian citizens after September 1, 1922. Italian-Canadian enemy aliens were required to register and report periodically to government offices. They were not allowed to leave Canada without permission and they could not assemble in groups of five or more people. Italian organizations that were considered Fascist, such as Case d'Italia, Dopolavoro, Fasci Italiani all'Estero, were declared illegal, shut down, and their property was confiscated by the government. On the very day that war was declared, police began to round up hundreds of people of Italian descent whose names were on lists prepared by the RCMP.

Declaration of War

Prime Minister Mackenzie King announcing Canada's declaration of war on Italy. In his speech, he also announces the internment of Italian Canadians. This was followed by publication of the internment order in the official *Canada Gazette*, pictured here.

Prime Minister William Lyon Mackenzie King:
"The Minister of Justice has authorized the Royal Canadian Mounted Police to take steps to intern all residents of Italian origin whose activities have given ground for the belief or reasonable suspicion that they might in time of war endanger the safety of the state or engage in activities prejudicial to the prosecution of the war . . ."
— June 10, 1940, CBC Radio address available at http://tinyurl.com/8vpylxr. The internment announcement is at 2:41 into the recording.

Shock and fear
It was a terrible nightmare for many Italian-Canadian men who were arrested the night of June 10, 1940. This distraught man was arrested in Windsor.

Unannounced
These RCMP officers were about to raid the Casa d'Italia in Toronto on June 10, 1940.

Dopolavoro hit too
The after-work clubs, the Dopolavoro, were also raided since they were essentially set up by the Italian consuls and were considered Fascist social clubs.

Leaving in a hurry
Two female employees leave Casa d'Italia in Toronto after it was raided.

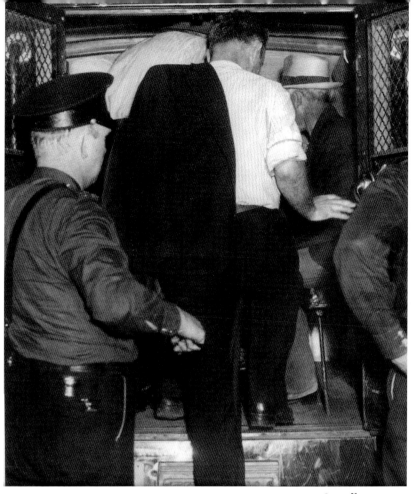

Benny Ferri:
    "The guards at the
    CNE marched us around
    outside, so the
    people could see us.
    I'll never forget how
    I felt. The people
    shouted at us and
    they threw garbage at
    us. The next day they
    put me on a train
    and shipped me out to
    Petawawa."

Loading up

Windsor police rounded up a load of targeted members of the Italian community and hauled them to the local jail in a paddy wagon.

 Watch Toni Ciccarelli describe her experience being taken away by the RCMP from her job at the post office, fingerprinted, and told she was a Fascist at tinyurl.com/internment6 (Segment #5)

Taken away

Some of the men being taken away by police didn't have a chance to say goodbye to their families. Note the children running along behind.

Arrested on-site

Most men were arrested on June 10, 1940, like this one below in Toronto. However, others were picked up during the summer. Benny Ferri was twenty-five years old when he was arrested on August 19, 1940, at International Harvester, where he worked. Police took him to the local jail in Hamilton and to the CNE grounds the next day.

Italian Canadians Become Enemy Aliens   59

Targeted for Internment

In the years before the war, the RCMP maintained a list of people whom they considered potential security risks. The list included Italian Fascists, especially those who held leadership positions in their local community organizations and clubs. The RCMP also collected the names of German pro-Nazis, communists, organized crime members, Canadian Nazis and fascists, and labour union leaders. Once war against Germany was declared in 1939, the Defence of Canada Regulations allowed the RCMP to arrest and imprison people without charging them with any crime, or allowing them legal counsel, or giving them a "day in court." This was called internment.

The RCMP began their roundup of German potential troublemakers before war was officially declared. By March 1940, 16,000 Canadian residents of German citizenship were declared enemy aliens and 847 (out of about 500,000) were interned.

Undercover agents had joined organizations to help make the list of targeted individuals, but most of the police information regarding Italian Fascists was collected from informants within the Italian-Canadian community. When war on Italy was declared, the RCMP and provincial police forces were ready to arrest a long list of community members. Within hours of the declaration of war, men were arrested and taken from their homes and businesses. Often they were not told where they were going. Families did not know that they wouldn't see these men for months or even years. Many were held in local jails, transferred to temporary prisons on the Canadian National Exhibition grounds in Toronto for holding, or put directly on trains to internment camps.

Prominent member of society
In 1939, Daniel Iannuzzi Sr. and his wife were invited to sit at the table of the Queen Mother during a royal tour. One year later he was interned as an enemy alien.

Watch Mary Thornton describe her experiences as a girl when the RCMP appeared and ransacked her home as she and her mother watched at tinyurl.com/internment7 (Segment #3, Segment #7)

Taken away from work
Daniel Iannuzzi Sr., seen here on his press pass/ID card issued by the city of Montreal police department in 1937, was working at his office at Casa d'Italia in Montreal when he was arrested. His son, Daniel Jr., went to the office after his school day was finished. He arrived to see two plainclothes RCMP officers arresting his father and putting him in a car. Young Daniel joined them in the car and they were taken to their home. His father was allowed to have dinner and get some things together. Another son, Paul, remembers watching his dad shave while the officers looked on. The RCMP said that they were taking him in for questioning. The family didn't see him again for two years, when he was released from internment.

"Within hours of the declaration of war, men were arrested and taken from their homes and businesses."

Frank Zaffiro, Hamilton

Frank Zaffiro of Hamilton, pictured here, was the Assistant Grand Venerable of the Sons of Italy of Ontario. That was one of the few groups that was not outlawed even during the war. A shoe repairman, Zaffiro was also active in a local Fascist political group.

▶ Watch Fernada Colangelo as she talks about the role of informants in creating fear in the Italian community and targeting individuals for arrest by the RCMP at tinyurl.com/internment8 (Segment #14)

Nick Zaffiro:
"My Dad was secretary of the Fascio. He was the head man. That's why he was interned. He didn't commit any crimes. He believed in Fascism in Italy and that Mussolini did a lot of good for the country. But here in Canada his politics were Liberal. It was the party in power when they immigrated here. The Conservatives didn't have many minorities in their party at the time."

34 months

Nick Zaffiro was ten years old and in grade five in Hamilton when he routinely reported after school to his father's shoe repair shop with his two sisters. On June 10, 1940, his father was not in the shop. The other kids in the area told him, "The police came and took your father away." Some added: "Your father's a spy." Frank was in prison for thirty-four months.

Co-worker accused him of spying

Michele LaPenna immigrated to Canada in 1911 and worked at the steel plant in Whitney Pier, Nova Scotia. He was arrested in 1940 along with several others. Michele suspected that someone at the steel plant had spoken to authorities and accused him of being an Italian spy in order to take his job.

Mayor of Montreal interned

Camillien Houde greets King George VI and Queen Elizabeth at Mont Royal in Montreal in 1939. Prime Minister Mackenzie King is on the left. Houde was mayor of Montreal from 1942 to 1948. Houde was not a Fascist or of Italian descent, but he praised Mussolini's Italy and its policies in his campaigns — it helped him win the Italian vote. Houde also donated municipal land for the construction of the Casa d'Italia social club in Montreal. For his generosity he received a knighthood from the Italian king. Houde vigorously openly opposed the federal government's conscription policy during the war. Many Quebecers fought conscription. With his political influence and large following in Quebec, the Canadian federal government considered Houde a threat to their war effort. He was interned.

> "Michele suspected that someone at the steel plant had spoken to authorities and accused him of being an Italian spy in order to take his job."

Gotcha!

Rocco Perri, seen here, was a leading crime boss in the Hamilton area. He was involved in bootlegging, drug smuggling, and other illegal businesses. The Hamilton police force had been tracking Perri for years but had been unable to convict him of any crimes. The roundup of Italian enemy aliens provided an easy solution to this problem. Police arrested him under the powers of the *War Measures Act* and interned him without a trial, like all other internees. At least sixteen other suspected organized crime figures from Hamilton, Guelph, and Niagara Falls were arrested and sent off to internment. Police were able to get them off the street without having to go through the courts.

Life Becomes Harder

Once Canada and Italy were at war, everything changed for Italian Canadians. People of Italian descent were openly subjected to racial slurs and even violence. Many were fired from their jobs. Italian business owners lost customers. Schoolchildren were bullied or ignored by their friends. In some cases, families had to move because their neighbours made life so unpleasant.

I'm interned
Families were not always told that their husbands and fathers had been taken away to internment camps. Some simply received a notice of internment, like this one, telling them where their loved one was.

> FORM I.O. 13
>
> C.P. Express
>
> I have been interned under the Defence of Canada Regulations. I will write you more details soon.
>
> Address my letters:
>
> c/o INTERNMENT OPERATIONS, Petawawa Ont
> Department of the Secretary of State,
> OTTAWA, Ontario.
>
> Date June 14, 1940
>
> Signature
>
> (Nothing except signature and date are to be written on this side.)

Vandalism
These children are looking at a broken fruit and vegetable store window on St. Clair Avenue West in Toronto. Many Italian businesses were targeted by vandals.

George Iantorno:

"My two sisters arrived home from work crying and upset because they had been fired from their jobs. Helen worked at General Electric and Josephine worked in a clothing factory on Spadina Avenue. They were both told that unless they could prove they or their father was a Canadian citizen they would be fired. The whole family was upset about the potential loss of family income and the fact that my sisters were being fired basically because of their ethnicity."

Lost their jobs
George Iantorno's sisters, Helen and Josephine, are shown here with a group of girlfriends in a photo taken in Toronto in about 1942. In the back row is Helen, first girl from the right, and Josephine is the third from the right.

Neighbourhoods changed
George Iantorno attended Dovercourt Public School during the war. He remembers that his neighbourhood changed for the worse after war was declared. "We had rocks thrown through our window and our door was broken by a boulder thrown by a kid in the neighbourhood. After one incident, my father went out and grabbed the offender and marched him down the street to his parents' house. My father knocked on the door of this house. He told the British-accented father what the son had done. The father pulled the kid inside and slammed the door in my Dad's face. No apology was offered."

Fairweather friends
Rose Papalia Santagato was sixteen when Mussolini declared war on the Allies. "It was a crazy time. My most vivid memory is of my best friend who I used to walk to school with. She was English Canadian. Every time Italy was mentioned, she let me know she disapproved of Italy in no uncertain terms. It was not so much in words but in her actions and attitude. My friend got real funny with snide remarks, a roll of the eyes, whatever. I definitely knew something was wrong with Italy and I was Italian. I felt uncomfortable."

WATCH THE VIDEO

Fired from the force
On the right is Nereo Brombal, a Windsor policeman who was fired in 1940 because he was Italian.

Watch Doug Brombal talk about his father Nereo Brombal's experiences at tinyurl.com/internment9

> "The reason that he is not a member of this Department now is on account of his being of Italian birth."

Some spoke out
This is a letter of support from Windsor's chief constable for Nereo Brombal, written after he was fired from the force because he was Italian.

City of Windsor

CLAUDE RENAUD
CHIEF CONSTABLE

POLICE DEPARTMENT

WINDSOR, ONTARIO

July 4, 1940.

To Whom It May Concern: Re: Nero Brombal.

This is to certify that I have known the above-named for the past 12 years, he being a member of this Department, which he has served faithfully.

The reason that he is not a member of this Department now is on account of him being of Italian birth.

Anything that you can do to assist this man will be appreciated by me.

Yours truly,

C. Renaud,
Chief Constable.

CR/WM

"Look at Eleanor, she's donating twenty-five cents and she's Italian!"

She's Italian!
Eleanor Mogavero Loreti, pictured here in her Girl Guide uniform in 1941, remembers her teacher announcing to the class during a Red Cross drive, "Look at Eleanor, she's donating twenty-five cents and she's Italian!" Eleanor was born in Toronto. When the teacher made that comment, Eleanor didn't know if she should be happy or sad. The teacher had praised her for her donation, yet had set her apart from the rest of the class and reinforced her image as an enemy alien. Eleanor's two older brothers, Salvy and Joe, were in the Canadian Army at the time.

CHAPTER 6
INTERNMENT AND FORCED LABOUR

Camp Petawawa and KP4W

Approximately 600 men of Italian descent were sent to internment camps in Canada during the Second World War. In the West, men were sent to Kananaskis, a small camp in British Columbia. In the East, internees were sent to either Camp Petawawa in Ontario or Camp Ripples in New Brunswick. Four women of Italian descent were interned at the Kingston Prison for Women (KP4W). The length of internment varied from person to person. In many cases, men were released within a few months. Some had to stay longer — usually those who were deemed Fascist supporters. None of the internees, however, were ever charged with any wrongdoing.

▶ WATCH THE VIDEO

Internees

These Italian men were internees at Camp Petawawa. They are dressed in work clothes suitable for camp labour, such as cutting trees. The population of the camp included Italian men of every age, occupation, and profession. The internees included university students, thirteen doctors who had become Canadians, lawyers, notaries, engineers, journalists, writers, artists, teachers, musicians, chemists, business owners, chefs, contractors, ex-policemen, pharmacists, shoemakers, gangsters, four Protestant ministers, and one Catholic priest. Shown here from left to right are Mario Furini, Bert Gatto, unknown, Felice Martinello, and Michele Rannie.

▶ Watch Frank Martinello discuss the impact on his family at tinyurl.com/internment11

Prison-like atmosphere

As seen in this photo (opposite page), Camp Petawawa had the atmosphere of a prison. Internees were behind barbed wire and guards were posted every 200 metres to keep them there. When internees broke the camp's rules, they were disciplined in its prison barracks.

▶ Watch Antoinette Olivieri as she describes her husband as a 12-year-old and his experiences visiting his father as a prisoner at the CNE grounds in Toronto and then at Petawawa at tinyurl.com/internment12 (Segment #6)

▶ WATCH THE VIDEO

Targeted

This oil painting of internee Erminio Ghislieri was done by fellow Italian Canadian internee Vincenzo Poggi. Note that Ghislieri is wearing a prisoner uniform with a red bull's eye on his left arm. In the background another internee sits on a bench with a larger target on his back. The guard tower in the background houses a guard who would be ready to shoot at the targets on the prisoners' uniforms if they tried to escape.

▶ Watch Maurice Poggi discuss his father, Vincenzo Poggi, and his experience painting in the camps and artwork during the war at tinyurl.com/internment13

"Christmas is close, daddy, and we want you home with your dear family. I musn't forget to tell you keep your chin up. I'll send my kisses to you. Your dear daughter, Lecha"

Interned because of a photo

Vito Peralta, pictured here, was interned for two years. When Windsor police officers raided a number of Italian homes on June 10, 1940, Mr. Peralta had a photo of his sons in their Fascist youth organization uniforms sitting on a table. Even though he explained that all children in Italy had to belong to a Fascist youth group, the officers decided that Mr. Peralta was a threat and took him away.

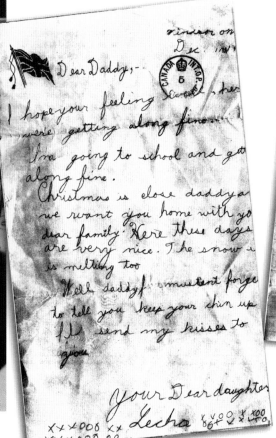

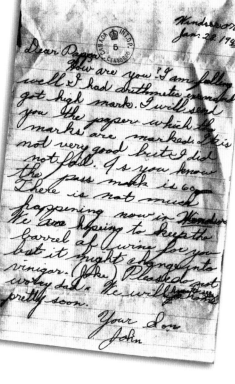

Letters to Papa

It was with mixed emotions that fathers received letters, like these ones, from their children. The pain of an internee's social isolation was immense, but many realized that the pain that their families went through without them as the breadwinner was greater. Many internees told stories of men crying while reading letters from home. The circular stamp on each letter is a mark made by the censor.

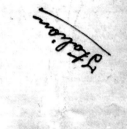

> "I told you that I need $10.00 per month for smoking and not only for smoking but also for shaving, haircut and many other little things you could image; I don't get any money if not from you. Now it is cold here, send me also salami and capocollo, they are good and some chicken. I would like to exchange with others. I am out of oil. If you send vegetables, pack also some oil."

ER OF WAR MAIL

My dearest wife . . .
Each month, internees were allowed to write three letters consisting of twenty-four lines and four postcards of eight lines each. Guards decided what words were considered offensive and the words were either cut out or blackened out from the letters. Letters were often full of requests for supplies to make life easier in the camps. The left-hand letter pictured here is written in Italian and the right-hand letter is a translation.

Letter sent by an Italian internee to his wife. The translation follows:
Lettera inviata da un internato italiano alla moglie. P10795A & B
Petawawa, Jan. 14, 1941

My Dearest Wife,

I like you to know that I have received your letter, which informs me of your good just as I can assure you about mine here. I understand from your letter that you, don't read well. I mentioned to you not to send me food that freezes, such as fruit vegetables. I have the rest. I already knew you would like that answer.

Try to believe in the devil and you'll see things will soon change for the better. I to that I need $10.00 per month for smoking and not only for smoking but also for s haircut and many other little things you could imagine; here I don't get any mone from you. Enough, I hope all is fine when you receive this letter. Now it is cold h me also salami and capocollo, they are good and some chicken. I would like to e with others. I am out of oil. If you send vegetables, pack also some oil. Today I r your $10.00, see I told you! I don't know why you tell me you are tired of this life you look back, you will see many people in worse conditions. Have hope and fai who is above all, even Satan. Therefore, take heart and don't forget on Feb. 9 to all together and receive communion. I receive it here every day. This is truly a r Hence, take care of yourself because when you have health you have everything. you know what it means to be sick. Please give my regards to all and tell that I r write to everyone. Give my regards to my brothers, sisters and brothers-in-law g to our children and Enes! Kiss on the nose (?) and to you because you are upset.

P.S. to our best boy John XX O, and our best girl Licia XX OOOOO

Your most devoted husband _____
N. 812 P.W. Camp Petawawa, Ont.

Wooden cutlery
A workshop barracks was set up where internees practised their trades as ironworkers, cobblers, tailors, mechanics, electricians, and woodworkers. To pass the time, many internees used their talents to carve items out of wood. This wooden cutlery was made by Luigi DeGregorio who was initially interned in Camp Petawawa and then moved to Camp Ripples in 1942. He was interned for two and a half years. These items are part of the display at the New Brunswick Internment Camp Museum in Minto.

Luisa Guagneli interned
Luisa Guagneli was an active member of the women's Fascio. She also worked as a volunteer, spreading Fascist propaganda in the Italian schools of Niagara Falls. Luisa was forty-two years old when she was arrested. She was initially held in a Toronto jail for six weeks and then was sent to the KP4W. She was released after five months with no charges ever laid.

Watch Eugene William Guagneli (son of Luisa) discuss the experience of having his mother taken away at tinyurl.com/internment14

WATCH THE VIDEO

Camp Ripples

Camp Ripples, near Minto, New Brunswick, was the only internment camp in the Maritimes. It was originally a relief camp, a place where out-of-work men were housed during the Great Depression. From 1941 to 1945, it held German and Italian merchant marines, people of Italian descent who lived in Canada and were considered a threat by the government, and other Canadians who were considered "potential troublemakers." Some internees started out at Petawawa and ended up at Ripples. The camp was a fifty-eight-acre property; fifteen acres of that was the fenced-in prison area. Much of the outlying land was covered in forest, where the internees were sent to cut wood. Although many of the residents of Minto and surrounding area were aware of the prison camp and had interactions with some of the internees, most people in the Maritimes had no idea that there was an internment camp in New Brunswick.

Talented artists
Many of the internees painted scenes of the camp. Some of their paintings were given away as gifts to people in the community. This one was given to a guard who took coffee to the artist/internee when the guard was on duty.

Oscar Bendl
This painting represent part of a larger series of images of Camp Ripples that were painted by internee Oscar Bendl.

"The circle on the back was meant as a target for the guards to shoot at should anyone try to escape."

Scale model

In this scale model of the camp, on display at the New Brunswick Internment Camp Museum, some internees are reading the postings on the bulletin boards to find out where their work detail would be that day. Most of the work involved going into the forest and cutting the huge amounts of wood needed to fuel the wood stoves in the camp. Other jobs included helping in the kitchen, hospital, library, canteen, or barracks. Internees earned twenty cents a day for their labour. The other internees modelled here are doing mandatory physical training under the watchful eye of a guard.

Guard tower

In this view of the scale model, a tall, white guard tower is in one corner of the fenced-in area. Guards were posted at regular intervals along the fences to ensure that nobody left or entered the camp without permission.

Typical room
This display at the New Brunswick Internment Camp Museum features bunk beds and simple furniture in a small space. It was a difficult adjustment for men to go from their busy households full of family members to a tiny room shared with a stranger.

A sketch from an internee's diary. (Courtesy Gary Barasch)

Diary sketch
Some internees kept diaries of their time spent in the camp. This is a sketch from one man's diary, showing his room. It was used as the basis for the display room in the museum.

"No Italian-Canadian family was untouched. Each family had someone — a brother, father, uncle, cousin — in the internment camp."

Italian prisoners

Many internees did not know why they had been arrested and imprisoned. As Benny Ferri lamented, "Why should we be there? We still ask those questions today. I didn't do anything wrong. I was a Canadian citizen." They also didn't know when they would be released. Most just lived each day as it came, did their work, socialized with their fellow inmates, and hoped for the best.

Camp Ripples internees

Up to sixty men from Hamilton were interned. One of them was Frank Zaffiro, pictured here at Camp Ripples in the middle of the back row. According to his son Nick, "No Italian-Canadian family was untouched. Each family had someone — a brother, father, uncle, cousin — in the internment camp."

Kitchen staff

The dining hall was serviced by a small army of cooks, pictured here. The internees missed their familiar Italian cuisine and often requested food from their families. Dan Iannuzzi Jr. recalls his father's story about the cooking at camp: "At Camp Petawawa the internees sent the kitchen staff away and they brought in Italian cooks who had been interned to cook the types of food that they liked."

At all the internment camps, food was important for the internees – and so were sports. Watch Attilio Girardi as he describes his father's experiences at the Kananaskis camp where Italian and German internees laboured on public works for the government at tinyurl.com/internment15 (Segment #9)

"The internees sent the kitchen staff away and they brought in Italian cooks who had been interned to cook the types of food that they liked."

Guards at Ripples
Most of the guards at Camp Ripples were veterans of the First World War who had tried to enlist but were not accepted. Instead, they were put on the Veterans Guard roster. There were 350 guards but they were rotated among the other camps in Canada, so they would not become too familiar or personally connected to any of the internees.

CHAPTER 7
WARTIME FAMILY LIFE FOR ITALIAN CANADIANS

A Broken Community

The whole Italian community felt the stigma of being "the enemy" in Canada. The community's leadership was torn apart by internment. Life was difficult without the Italian-speaking doctors, lawyers, businessmen, teachers, and tradesmen who had been taken away. Those who were left behind got the message that to organize or complain meant they could be taken away, too. For some, even speaking Italian became suspect. They were often told to speak English at work, even amongst themselves, because others feared they were plotting something. An unwarranted sense of shame fell upon the community.

Families on their own
Ida Pataracchia is shown with her daughter, Enrica. Enrica was five years old when her father was taken away. It was nearly impossible for such small children to understand what had happened and why. All they knew was that their papas were gone, their mamas were very sad and worried, and life had changed for the worse.

 Watch Mary Thornton as she describes how her family changed their name to avoid trouble and help Mary get a job at tinyurl.com/internment16 (Segment #3)

Dear father . . .
These are letters from the Pataracchia children to their father, Nello, who was interned at Camp Ripples.

Postcards home
Nello Pataracchia sent these postcards dated October 21, 1942 (right) and September 23, 1944 (below) to his wife, Ida. There was a limit of four postcards per month per internee.

Glory days
Nello Pataracchia had a good life before internment.

"The family is sad because you are not at home for Christmas and I hope you will be home before New Years . . ."

It was hell!
Romano Scattolon, pictured here, was a coal miner in Glace Bay, Nova Scotia, when he was interned. His teenaged son, Londo, tells what it was like to be left alone: "The authorities didn't care about the families of the men in the camp. Who was going to feed me and my mother and my two brothers? We were also in constant fear. People were throwing rocks at our house; it was hell! When you come to look at it, by gees, it was terrible, wasn't it? I mean, my dad loved Canada."

▶ Watch Geno Scattolon (son of Romano) talk about his family's experience at tinyurl.com/internment17

▶ WATCH THE VIDEO

Parties banned

Before the war with Italy was declared in June, Italian weddings, like this one in 1940 between James and Ann Cavalluzzo, were big affairs. Once the *War Measures Act* was activated, Italian Canadians were not allowed to gather in groups larger than five, so weddings like this were impossible. Jenny and Rocco Tamburro are seen here in the front row as the flower girl and ring bearer. They remember being verbally abused on the way to and from school and in the schoolyard. Some kids were prevented from joining school clubs and teams because of their Italian names. "They picked on us . . . We were very stigmatized by these experiences, but we survived school, the taunts of our Canadian peers, and the war," said Rocco, who grew up to be a doctor.

"Some kids were prevented from joining school clubs and teams because of their Italian names."

A sympathetic teacher

This picture features Italian-Canadian children at St. Anthony School in Ottawa's Little Italy in 1938. They were celebrating Christmas. Life was hard for these children but some teachers helped to make it better. Italo Tiezzi recalled a teacher who kept her eye on the boys at the school to make sure they weren't being bothered. It wasn't just other children who acted against them. When his brother, Silvio, was picked as the best entry in a school-sponsored public speaking contest, the judges decided that he couldn't win because his father was interned.

▶ WATCH THE VIDEO

Bullied for being Italian

John Edward De Toro, pictured here, was a teen the day war broke out with Italy. He was exiting his school when three older kids started pushing him around and punching him. They accused "his people" of killing "their people." From that day forward, he ran home from school to avoid being beaten up and called derogatory names. Finally, his dad spoke to the principal who then put a stop to the bullying.

▶ Watch John Edward De Toro discuss bullying and how he was treated at school at tinyurl.com/internment18

Not a very merry Christmas

Being away from family during important religious holidays, such as Christmas, was especially hard. This holiday postcard was sent by internees at Camp Ripples to their families. The illustration of thin men with targets on their backs doesn't look all that jolly. The cards were printed by The War Prisoners' Aid of the YMCA.

Merry Xmas
Happy New Year

Printed by The War Prisoners' Aid of the Y.M.C.A.

Suddenly Poor

For families of internees, life was very difficult after their breadwinner was taken away from them. Other Italians lost their incomes when they were fired from their jobs or laid off because they were of Italian descent. Those who ran businesses lost many of their customers because people refused to support anything Italian. Italian families were no longer eligible for social assistance. Mayor Day of Toronto said, "Italians cannot very well expect us to spend money on them when we need it for the war effort." Many were forced to rely on family and friends and whatever work they could find. A lot of children had to quit school to earn money for their families while their fathers were unemployed or interned. Some families lost their businesses and their homes because they didn't have the money to maintain them. Future dreams for higher education and businesses were put on hold.

Getting even

Dan Iannuzzi Jr.'s mother had to raise six children under the age of fourteen. They are pictured here with their grandmother and an unidentified friend. Their father was the editor and publisher of *L'Italia*, an Italian-language newspaper in Montreal. When he was interned, the family's print shop was confiscated by the authorities. It burned down one night. Because of the internment, the insurance policy was no longer valid and there was no money to rebuild the shop. No one was ever charged for setting the fire.

"That's the type of thing people did to you then," said Dan. "Deface your property, set fires, and so on . . . to get even for the fact that their neighbours of course were Italian."

Paul Iannuzzi, pictured here on the bicycle, remembers that he and his mother appeared before a judge to see if they could get financial help of some kind. "We didn't receive a cent from the Canadian government. We were told we were enemies of the country." They were all born in Canada except for his mother, who had emigrated from Italy when she was two years old. However, at the meeting, Paul remembers something good happening, too. "An RCMP officer slipped me a fifty cent piece in my hand because he must've felt sorry for us."

WATCH THE VIDEO

Eighteen and in charge

Kay Costantini, pictured here second from the left in the front row, was eighteen years old when her father, Joe, was taken away by the RCMP in Ottawa and interned. Since her mother had died two years before, Kay became the mother figure and the father figure to her younger brothers and sister. She took on the running of the household and trying to pay the bills.

Watch Gloria Costantini Giroux (sister of Kay Costantini), who was a child at the time of internment, discuss her family situation after her father was interned and the role her older sister played at tinyurl.com/internment19

"A lot of children had to quit school to earn money for their families while their fathers were unemployed or interned."

Mothers go out to work

Although it was not common for women to work at jobs outside the home, when their husbands were fired or interned, many women were forced to leave their families and earn a paycheque. There was no social assistance for Italian families. When seven-year-old Italo Tiezzi's father was interned, life became much harder. His mother, pictured here with Italo and his brother, Silvio (on the left), had to get a job to help support her family. She managed to find work at the Mayfair Pie Bakery in Ottawa for eight dollars a week — barely enough to survive on.

Sal Pantalone was fifteen when his father, Fred, pictured here in his firefighter's uniform, was arrested at work in front of his co-workers and interned. "My mother scratched and scraped to maintain the household. For additional income of twenty-five dollars a month, we rented the second story of our house. The main family income had ceased; my two older brothers contributed what they could. When I turned sixteen, I faked my age and joined the navy. From my forty dollar monthly pay, I was able to send home thirty dollars."

"When I turned sixteen, I faked my age and joined the navy. From my forty dollar monthly pay, I was able to send home thirty dollars."

▶ Watch Elio Salciccioli describe his experiences as a boy watching the RCMP raid his home; his father, a Hamilton steelworker, was locked out of his job until he was cleared by the RCMP at tinyurl.com/internment20 (Segment #4)

Had to quit school

Nick Zaffiro was ten when his father, Frank, was taken to an internment camp, where he was held for nearly three years. "My oldest sister, Lil, was thirteen and in grade eight and she had to quit school to go to work to help the family." Nick is pictured here with his mother and Lil in the back, and his two younger sisters, Antionette and Frances. After his father was interned, there were shoes left in his store to be repaired. "My mother told me take them to another shoemaker in the north end to be fixed. I got a twenty dollar bill to take to my mother. There were a lot of bills to pay. As a kid of ten, I went to the bank to get the twenty-dollar bill changed into smaller bills. I thought it looked like more money that way." Nick also worked every night after school and on weekends at a local fish-and-chip shop. He contributed his wages to the family income.

WATCH THE VIDEO

Millionaire no more

Annie and James Franceschini pose here with their daughter, Myrtle, in 1930. James was a millionaire businessman and socialite before the war. After his internment, his successful construction businesses were sold by the government for far less than their value. Some companies and their equipment were sold to direct competitors, leading James to suspect that his internment was a result of jealousy amongst his business rivals. His estate home, horses, and plant collections were sold for next to nothing.

 Watch James McCreath discuss his grandfather James Franceschini's internment experience at tinyurl.com/internment3 (Link also appears on p. 16 and 35)

Sudbury loses a doctor

Dr. Luigi Pancaro practised in Sudbury until he was taken away and interned in June 1940. During his absence, his wife single-handedly supported and raised five children. To do this she rented out parts of the Pancaro home to boarders. Women who had been accustomed to hiring help for around the house found themselves doing all the chores on their own, including things like shovelling coal into the furnace.

"One day they worked shoulder-to-shoulder and the next day it was as if they were not just strangers, but enemies."

Luckier than most

Rose Papalia Santagato, pictured here at fourteen with a friend, was luckier than most Italians during the war. Her father ran a bakery called Queen City Bakery. "While Italian businesses may have been boycotted during the war because of anti-Italian discrimination, I don't think my dad's business was because it was largely an Italian clientele."

Miners refused to work

Many Italian Canadians lost their jobs after war was declared on Italy. In Dominion, Cape Breton, some of the non-Italian miners refused to work with Italians. One day they worked shoulder-to-shoulder and the next day it was as if they were not just strangers, but enemies. This caused work stoppages and some of the mines were closed for months. No work meant no pay, so families struggled to put food on the table. Eventually management arranged a settlement and work resumed. When the Italian miners went back to work, they were placed on the less desirable night shift.

Dominion No. 1 Colliery, Cape Breton, Canada.

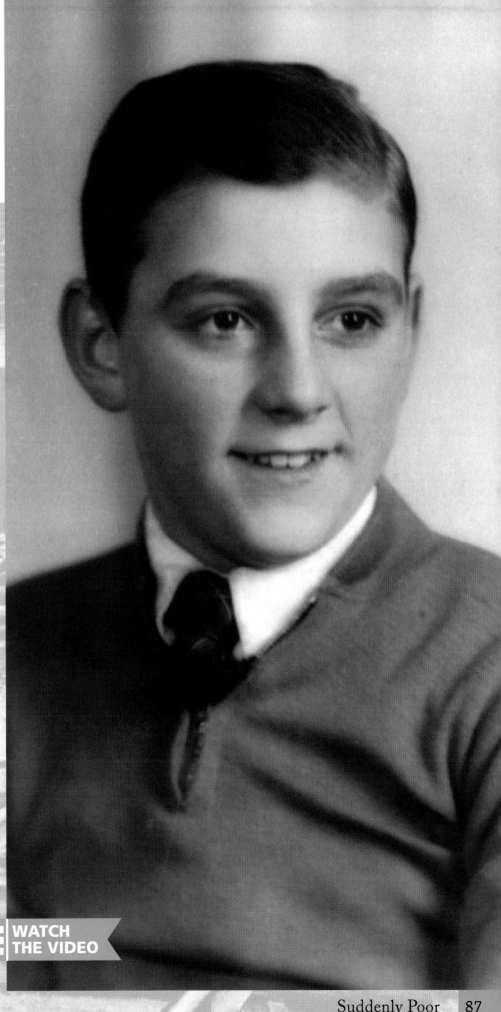

Kids went to work

Frank Martinello was twelve and living with his family in Sydney, Nova Scotia, when his father, Felice, was interned. His mother couldn't get a job to support them because she had seven children to look after. His oldest sister was sixteen and she had to quit school to work. His younger brothers delivered newspapers. Frank continued to attend school, but every day when it was finished, he took a bus to a friend of his father's who had a shoeshine shop. "I shined shoes from 3:30 pm until 7 pm five days a week and until 9 pm on Friday. On Saturday, I worked from early morning until 11 pm. I made pretty good money on tips whenever the American boats would come into Sydney. One Saturday I made thirty-five dollars on tips. That was a lot of money back then. My mother hugged and hugged me and kissed me when I handed over my money."

The Martinellos owned a house, but they were told by the government to sell it. "When you use up the money from the sale of the house, we will give you relief." The family thought they'd be in a worse financial state if they followed that advice.

Watch Frank Martinello discuss the impact on his family at tinyurl.com/internment22 (Link also appears on p. 69)

Frank Martinello:
"An egg and a slice of baloney was a good meal then. I was skin and bones. I didn't start to fatten up until after my dad got out of camp."

WATCH THE VIDEO

Arbitrary Release

Once the internees were locked up in the camps, the government began processing them to determine how much of a threat they were to the country, if any. They were interviewed and required to fill out forms committing their loyalties to Canada. Some were released in a few months, while others were kept for years. Who stayed and who got to go home often appeared to be a very arbitrary decision.

Dan Iannuzzi Jr.'s Uncle Frank was released because "they found out the only thing he did for Mussolini was play on the Dopolavoro baseball team." Those who admitted to being Fascist were kept the longest. In many cases, internees had a son serving in the Canadian Armed Forces. Often a man would be released from prison camp one week and drafted to fight for Canada the next!

None of the interned men were ever charged or convicted of any crimes. When a man was released, he was on parole and had to report monthly to his local RCMP office.

▶ WATCH THE VIDEO

Honourable Justice James Duncan Hyndman:

"In many of the cases, the parties were entirely incapable of doing the things alleged against them, and I might further add that I cannot recall a single instance in which any overt act or expression indicating subversive intentions was proved. The only evidence was as to membership in some organization, and as there are many hundreds who were members of these organizations still at large, I am inclined to think that mere membership cannot be regarded very seriously, even by the Police."

— Part of a letter from Honourable Justice James Duncan Hyndman, a former judge of Alberta's Supreme Court who was appointed to review the cases of internees who objected to their internment, to Minister of Justice, Ernest Lapointe, May 1, 1941.

Business as usual

Nello Pataracchia owned the Cabot Macaroni Manufacturing Company in Hamilton, Ontario. Even though Nello was interned, the Canadian government contracted with his company to supply pasta products to be served to internees at Camp Petawawa. This is just one of many examples where the government displayed hypocrisy in their dealings with Italian Canadians.

▶ Watch Attilio Girardi as he talks about his father's attempt at getting released, and the reliance of government authorities on secret informants whose information was often false at tinyurl.com/internment24 (Segment #19)

Domenic Nardocchio

Domenic Nardocchio, pictured on the left with a sketch done by a fellow internee at Petawawa, joined his father in Cape Breton, Nova Scotia, in 1916 at the age of twelve. He left school at fifteen to learn the shoemaking trade and by the age of twenty-four he had his own shop. He was in his shop when the police came to take him away in June 1940.

Domenic tells of the day in February 1941, when the RCMP officer at the camp told him, "Domenic, we're not going to see each other any more." Domenic said, "Why? What happened?" "Well," the officer said, "I am fully convinced that you people are no threat to the security of Canada. You people have been interned through jealousy of one another. You have informers, who have personal vendettas against you. They went to the RCMP and lied and said that you were a threat to Canada. But under this investigation I am fully convinced that you people should not be held any more. As far as I'm concerned, I'm going to make a recommendation to my superior that you all be released. If it was up to me," he said, "I'd send you back tomorrow."

The investigation did end, but Domenic was held there another thirteen months. He was finally released on March 8, 1942.

▶ Watch Dominic Nardocchio Jr. talk about his father's experience, including the RCMP's arbitrary failure to release him at tinyurl.com/internment23

Will you fight for us?

Benny Ferri was interned for eleven months at Camp Petawawa. When he appeared at his review hearing, he was asked by the judge if he would fight for Canada in the army. He said, "Yes, but just don't send me to the Italian front. I have a brother who is fighting for Italy. I wouldn't want to be in the position of having to shoot my brother over there." A month after Mr. Ferri was released, he received his conscription notice.

"One month I'm an enemy alien, the next I'm Canadian enough to be in the Canadian Army." This sketch of Benny Ferri was done by fellow internee Guido Cassini at Camp Petawawa.

Arbitrary Release   89

Life After Internment

Most Italian-Canadian internees were released before the end of the war. In some cases they were able to pick up where they left off. Others found it very difficult since they had a sense of guilt or embarassment regarding their internment. Many still couldn't understand why they had been singled out and they suspected that there had been local informants. Some men couldn't get their old jobs back. Felice Martinello was ordered not to go back to Nova Scotia. He was told he had to live in either Ontario or British Columbia. There was still a sense of fear amongst the Italian community and in some cases families and friends were afraid to associate with the released men in case the RCMP would arrest them, too.

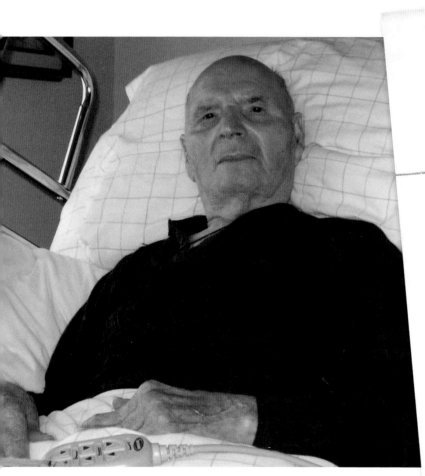

Ignored by family
Benny Ferri, pictured here at his nursing home in Hamilton, Ontario, in October 2008, was lucky to get his job back at International Harvester when he was released. "There was one guy at work who was kinda nasty to me. But I just didn't pay attention." However, he was hurt by the people who avoided talking to him, especially when one day his aunt and uncle ignored him on the street. "They were afraid of being seen talking to me in case they got into trouble somehow. Afraid someone would report them for talking to me."

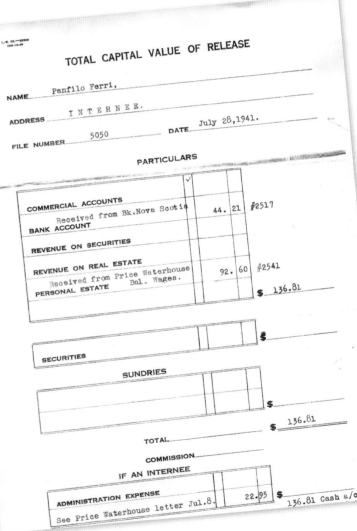

Poor pay
For his work with a pick and shovel on the roads outside the camp, Benny was paid twenty-five cents a day. When he was interned, the Custodian of Enemy Alien Property took the $44.00 he had in the bank and held it in trust. At the end of his internment, the accounting firm Peat Marwick charged Benny's account $22.95 for administering his account — a large fee for a small balance. Benny's capital release form is above.

WATCH THE VIDEO

Released due to illness

Millionaire James Franceschini is pictured here in *Who's Who in Canada, 1930–31*. He was eventually released from internment camp on medical grounds. The Custodian of Enemy Alien Property had taken over the administration of his companies. He grew despondent when he realized that the assets of his companies had been severely reduced under the watch of the Custodian. Some suspect that their poor administration was intentional. After the government sold most of his assets for rock-bottom prices, James grew more depressed. His internment also took a toll on his marriage. Few of his friends rallied to support him during this crisis, which hurt James. He could never forget his discriminatory treatment by the Canadian government and politicians. Yet, he always maintained pride in being Canadian and the opportunities the country provided him. He died in 1960 after rebuilding much of his empire.

Watch James McCreath discuss his grandfather James Franceschini's experience at tinyurl.com/internment3 (Link also appears on p. 16, 35, and 84)

Lost his job

Gino Tiezzi, second from left in the bottom row, was interned at Camp Petawawa. His son, Italo, recalls that both parents refused to sign declarations that would help to release him from the camp because they felt it was wrong, even if it meant he would have to stay in prison. When he was finally released, he could not get his job back as a meter reader inspector in Ottawa.

Loss of Canadian citizenship

John Nardocchio was six years old when he and his family came to Cape Breton. After the war, he decided he had better become a Canadian citizen so he went to the courthouse, signed the documents, and was sworn in. A month later he received a call from the citizenship office about his wife. "Mr. Nardocchio," said the man, "this may sound kind of out of place, but although your wife was born in Guysborough County and she's a Canadian, when she married you she lost her Canadian rights. Right now she's gotta get naturalized as a Canadian."

Life After Internment

> "He wasn't bitter. The only bad experience was his lost time with family and constantly worrying about us struggling financially."

Bounced back
Dan Iannuzzi Sr., front row, went on to found a successful multilingual newspaper and television presence in Canada. He died in 1992. The Iannuzzi family is still prominent in philanthropy and the multilingual media industry in Canada. The Iannuzzi family is pictured here on the occasion of their parents' twenty-fifth wedding anniversary.

You just move on

Ninetta Frenza's father was a shoemaker, but also volunteered as a secretary to the Order Sons of Italy at the Casa d'Italia in Montreal. Ninetta was fourteen when he was interned for twenty-two months. "They're memories which at the time were a little devastating, but when you're a teenager you don't feel that it's as devastating as it was for my mother . . . I knew she was having problems but when you're a teenager you don't take it the same way. You just move on." After his release he worked as a tailor and eventually opened a men's clothing retail shop. "He wasn't bitter. The only bad experience was his lost time with family and constantly worrying about us struggling financially." Leonardo is pictured here with sixteen-year-old Ninetta one month after his release.

▶ Watch Antonia Maria (Ninetta) Ricci, pictured here with her father, Leonardo Frenza, discuss her experience at tinyurl.com/internment26

Voted out of service

When Fred Pantalone was released from internment he wanted to return to his job as a firefighter in Ottawa. But the firefighter's union, his fellow firefighters, voted unanimously not to take him back into the service. He lost his pension, his career, and his professional community. To make ends meet he took jobs working overnight in a bakery and then as a taxi driver. Then Fred enlisted in the Canadian Navy and became a fire marshal at a large Canadian ammunition dump. He had a successful career in the navy and is pictured here in his navy uniform in 1943.

▶ Watch Joseph Mastromonaco as he eloquently describes the emotional impact on himself as a boy and later in life of the absence of his father due to the internment at tinyurl.com/internment27 (Segments #20, #22)

Life After Internment

Postwar Life for Italian Canadians

The shame and fear that lingered in the Italian-Canadian community after the war led some Italians to take on English forms of their names and deny their cultural roots. In Montreal and Toronto, many did not want to start up the old social clubs again since they had caused people to be interned. But when Canada changed its immigration policy and started to allow Italians back into the country, there was a huge influx of Italian immigrants. They moved into the cities and reinforced the Little Italies that had existed before the war. As the strength of cultural ties increased, the social groups started up again and expanded. While maintaining their culture, Italian Canadians also managed to integrate into mainstream Canadian society and establish successful professional careers and businesses. There are many examples of highly successful Canadians of Italian descent who have helped make Canada a better and more prosperous nation.

Coming to Canada
New generations of Italian immigrants are pictured on board the *Conte Bianca Maro*, en route from Genoa to Toronto in 1951.

New wave of immigrants
From 1947 to 1948, Canada revised its immigration policy with respect to Italians. That sparked a huge wave of Italian immigrants in the late 1940s and the 1950s.

Pier 21

Pier 21 in Halifax, Nova Scotia, was usually the first glimpse of Canada that new immigrants saw. These Italian children are being processed by Canadian immigration officers in Pier 21 in 1963.

Boxes of belongings

These images of Pier 21 in 1963 show piles of luggage owned by immigrants. Like the immigrants before them, Italians brought pieces of their lives from Italy, as well as their culture and their enthusiasm for starting a new life in Canada.

Postwar Life for Italian Canadians

Toronto
This 2012 photo of a street corner in Toronto's Little Italy illustrates a vibrant ethnic community with many successful businesses that Italians and non-Italians visit.

Winnipeg
Many Italian immigrants ended up in Winnipeg and established their own Little Italy there. This shot is of Corydon Avenue in 1991.

Windsor
The Via Italia on Erie Street in Windsor, Ontario, is the designated Italian area in the city. There are many Italian-Canadian businesses and it is known as a gourmet restaurant district. This is also the site of the St. Angela Merici Festival celebrations each August.

World Cup soccer celebration
Italy has won the World Cup for soccer several times. After each win, thousands of Italian Canadians fill the streets in cities around the world. This Toronto celebration was for the victory in 1984, proving that the Italian-Canadian community is alive and thriving.

Ottawa
An eye-catching mural under a bridge marks Ottawa's Little Italy.

NHL stars
Former National Hockey League star Tony Esposito was a Hall-of-Famer, as was his brother, Phil. Roberto Luongo, former captain of the Vancouver Canucks, is also of Italian heritage and has a star on Toronto's Italian Walk of Fame, along with many other famous Canadians of Italian descent.

The magazine with an Italian accent
A number of newspapers and magazines are published by the Italian-Canadian community, some in English and some in Italian. *Accenti* is published in Montreal by Domenic Cusmano and celebrates Italian culture and successes. This issue sparked discussion about their wrongful treatment in the past.

Order of Canada
Lino Magagna obtained a doctoral degree from the University of Toronto, was founder of the National Congress of Italian Canadians, and is a member of the Order of Canada.

Top judge

The Hon. Frank Iacobucci is a former justice of the Supreme Court of Canada. He has received over a dozen honorary university degrees and was appointed a Companion in the Order of Canada in July 2007. He now works for a major law firm in Toronto.

Watch Frank Iacobucci discuss his family's experience during the Second World War at tinyurl.com/internment28

Acclaimed author

Nino Ricci was born in Leamington, Ontario, to parents from the Molise region of Italy. He completed university studies in Toronto, Montreal, and Florence, Italy. He is a highly successful, award-winning author, including two Governor General's Awards. Mr. Ricci lives in Toronto.

WATCH THE VIDEO

Il Postino

Ottawa's *Il Postino* is published by the Preston Street Community Foundation, an Italian-Canadian community centre located in the capital region. It prints articles in Italian, English, and French.

Union leader

Ken Georgetti is from Trail, BC. His career has taken him from pipefitter to shop steward to president of the Canadian Labour Congress and founder of labour-owned, multi-million-dollar companies. He has been awarded the Order of Canada and the Order of British Columbia.

Postwar Life for Italian Canadians 99

CHAPTER 9
ACKNOWLEDGING THE PAST

Apologies

In 1988, Prime Minister Brian Mulroney officially apologized to all Japanese Canadians for their internment during the Second World War and agreed upon a redress package for individuals and the community. Following this apology, the National Congress of Italian Canadians (NCIC) sought an apology from the government for the injustices done to people of Italian descent during the war. Prime Minister Mulroney eventually made an apology to a group of Italian Canadians in 1990, but it was outside of Parliament so it is not considered "official" by many people.

In his apology, the prime minister acknowledged that none of the Italian internees were ever charged or convicted of any crimes. Afterwards, the Italian-Canadian Redress Committee put pressure on the government to provide compensation for those who were interned. In 2005, an agreement was reached between Prime Minister Paul Martin and the Italian-Canadian community represented by several major organizations. They reached a financial settlement to be administered through the NCIC Foundation.

When Stephen Harper became prime minister the following year, he withdrew the offer and created the Community Historical Recognition Program (CHRP). This provided the Italian-Canadian community with much less money and no control over it. Pal Di Iulio, the CEO of Villa Charities in Toronto, was appointed Chair of the CHRP Italian community committee with members from across Canada. The committee received applications from the community to "acknowledge, commemorate and educate" the public on the internment issue. The committee reviewed and recommended projects and the Minister of Citizenship and Immigration made all the final decisions on funding proposed projects from Halifax to Vancouver.

In 2010, Liberal MP Massimo Pacetti introduced Bill C-302, which asked for a formal apology in Parliament, a $2.5 million fund to produce educational materials related to Italian-Canadian history, and a commemorative stamp to be issued by Canada Post. It was passed in the House of Commons by all parties except the Conservatives and went on to the Senate, where it died when a new election was called.

The Italian-Canadian community does not agree on whether or not they should keep up their fight for redress. Some think it is time to move on, while others cannot forget the humiliation and injustices of the past.

Watch Giulette Doganieri talk about the shame she felt about her father being interned and how she felt she could not talk about it to her children and others at tinyurl.com/internment29 (Segment #7)

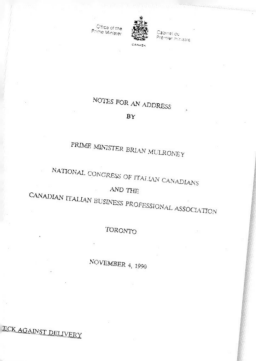

NOTES FOR AN ADDRESS

BY

PRIME MINISTER BRIAN MULRONEY

NATIONAL CONGRESS OF ITALIAN CANADIANS
AND THE
CANADIAN ITALIAN BUSINESS PROFESSIONAL ASSOCIATION

TORONTO

NOVEMBER 4, 1990

ECK AGAINST DELIVERY

The prime minister's apology

The text of the official apology that Prime Minister Brian Mulroney offered to Italian Canadians on November 4, 1990 in Toronto:

Brian Mulroney, page 4, paragraph 5 of speech:
"None of the 700 internees was ever charged with an offence and no judicial proceedings were launched. It was often, in the simplest terms, an act of prejudice — organized and carried out under law, but prejudice nevertheless."

Brian Mulroney, page 5 of speech:
"On behalf of the government and people of Canada, I offer a full and unqualified apology for the wrongs done to our fellow Canadians of Italian origin during World War II."

Making amends

Prime Minister Brian Mulroney speaking with Frank Zaffiro, who was interned for thirty-four months without charges, at the event where he delivered his apology for the internment.

Continuing the fight

Liberal MP Massimo Pacetti introduced Bill C-302, the proposed Italian-Canadian Recognition and Restitution Act, in 2010. He is pictured here speaking about his proposed legislation in Parliament. Although the bill died in the Senate when a new election was called, he says he may be willing to reintroduce it if he receives renewed and increased support from the Italian-Canadian community.

Permanent Acknowledgements

Across the country, museums, memorials, books, and other materials have been created to acknowledge the Italian Canadian internment in the Second World War. Through the Community Historical Recognition Program, a number of projects were funded to help educate the public about this historical wrong.

"A local teacher began an excavation project at the site of Camp Ripples with the help of twelve at-risk students."

Students helped create a museum
Ed Caissie, pictured here at the New Brunswick Internment Camp Museum in Minto, New Brunswick, began an excavation project at the site of Camp Ripples with the help of twelve at-risk students. The project eventually grew to include over sixty students and involved building a scale model of the fifty-eight-acre camp and its fifty-two buildings, which is a prized feature of the museum's exhibits.

CONSTABLE NEREO BROMBAL
1897 - 1974

THIS PLAQUE IS ERECTED
TO THE MEMORY
OF CONSTABLE NEREO BROMBAL, A NATIVE OF
CAERANO DI SAN MARCO IN THE PROVINCE OF TREVISO
IN THE NORTH KINGDOM OF ITALY
WHOSE 12 YEARS OF SERVICE WITH THE DEPARTMENT OF POLICE
FOR THE CITY OF WINDSOR WAS UNJUSTLY TERMINATED
IN THE MONTH OF JUNE 1940
BECAUSE OF HIS PLACE OF BIRTH.

THE BOARD OF COMMISSIONERS OF POLICE
FOR THE CITY OF WINDSOR
AND THE WINDSOR POLICE SERVICE ACKNOWLEDGE
WITH GRATITUDE THE WORK OF CONSTABLE BROMBAL AND
THEIR DEEP REGRET FOR THE INJUSTICE DONE TO HIM AND
OTHERS OF THE ITALIAN COMMUNITY AT A TIME WHEN REASON
AND HUMANITY HAD BEEN ABANDONED.

WATCH THE VIDEO

Windsor apology

On December 12, 1990, the Windsor Police Commission officially apologized to the family of Nereo Brombal, a police officer who was fired from the Windsor Police Force because of his Italian heritage when Canada declared war on Italy. This plaque was presented to Nereo's son, Douglas Brombal, in Windsor to commemorate the apology. Part of the text on the plaque is "The Board of Commissioners of Police for the City of Windsor and the Windsor Police Service acknowledge with gratitude the work of Constable Brombal and their deep regret for the injustice done to him and others of the Italian community at a time when reason and humanity had been abandoned."

Watch Doug Brombal talk about his father's experiences at tinyurl.com/internment9 (Link also appears on p. 66)

PIAZZA DANTE Memorial Wall

This Memorial Wall is a testament to the Italian Canadians of Ottawa for their perseverance, courage and loyalty to Canada during the Second World War.
(1939-1945)

With Italy's declaration of war against the Allied forces on June 10, 1940, Canadians of Italian origin were declared enemy aliens. Thousands of men and women across Canada were required to report to the Royal Canadian Mounted Police. Though no charges were laid against them, approximately 630 people of Italian origin were sent to internment camps. Five Ottawa men were interned in camps in Petawawa, Ontario and Gagetown, New Brunswick.

Italian Canadians in Ottawa participated fully in supporting Canada's war effort. Many served in Canada's armed forces. Among them a number died overseas fighting for their country

Internees Include
Giuseppe Costantini
Fred R. Pantalone
Vittorio Sabetta
Carlo Scarabelli
Gino Tiezzi

Died in the Line of Duty
Anthony Barbaro
Domenic Calderone
Adrian Girolami
Frank Prosperine
Alfred Menchini

Memorial Wall

This Memorial Wall was unveiled in Dante Park, Ottawa, Ontario, in 2011. It is "a testament to the Italian Canadians of Ottawa for their perseverance, courage, and loyalty to Canada during the Second World War." It names five local members of the Italian community who were interned, as well as six others who died in the line of duty.

Monument to multiculturalism

This sculpture stands in front of Union Station in Toronto. It was erected by the local Italian-Canadian community in 1985 as a tribute to multiculturalism.

Permanent Acknowledgements

Timeline

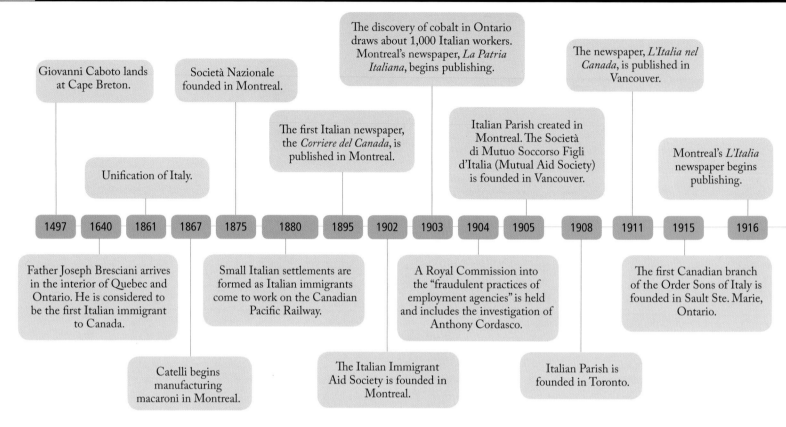

Giovanni Caboto lands at Cape Breton.

Società Nazionale founded in Montreal.

The discovery of cobalt in Ontario draws about 1,000 Italian workers. Montreal's newspaper, *La Patria Italiana*, begins publishing.

The newspaper, *L'Italia nel Canada*, is published in Vancouver.

The first Italian newspaper, the *Corriere del Canada*, is published in Montreal.

Italian Parish created in Montreal. The Società di Mutuo Soccorso Figli d'Italia (Mutual Aid Society) is founded in Vancouver.

Montreal's *L'Italia* newspaper begins publishing.

Unification of Italy.

1497 1640 1861 1867 1875 1880 1895 1902 1903 1904 1905 1908 1911 1915 1916

Father Joseph Bresciani arrives in the interior of Quebec and Ontario. He is considered to be the first Italian immigrant to Canada.

Small Italian settlements are formed as Italian immigrants come to work on the Canadian Pacific Railway.

A Royal Commission into the "fraudulent practices of employment agencies" is held and includes the investigation of Anthony Cordasco.

The first Canadian branch of the Order Sons of Italy is founded in Sault Ste. Marie, Ontario.

Catelli begins manufacturing macaroni in Montreal.

The Italian Immigrant Aid Society is founded in Montreal.

Italian Parish is founded in Toronto.

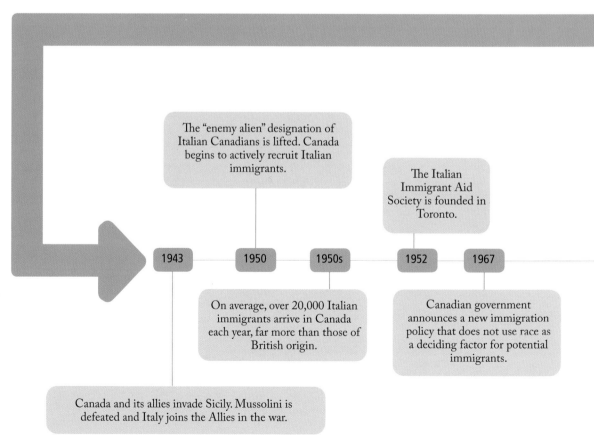

The "enemy alien" designation of Italian Canadians is lifted. Canada begins to actively recruit Italian immigrants.

The Italian Immigrant Aid Society is founded in Toronto.

1943 1950 1950s 1952 1967

On average, over 20,000 Italian immigrants arrive in Canada each year, far more than those of British origin.

Canadian government announces a new immigration policy that does not use race as a deciding factor for potential immigrants.

Canada and its allies invade Sicily. Mussolini is defeated and Italy joins the Allies in the war.

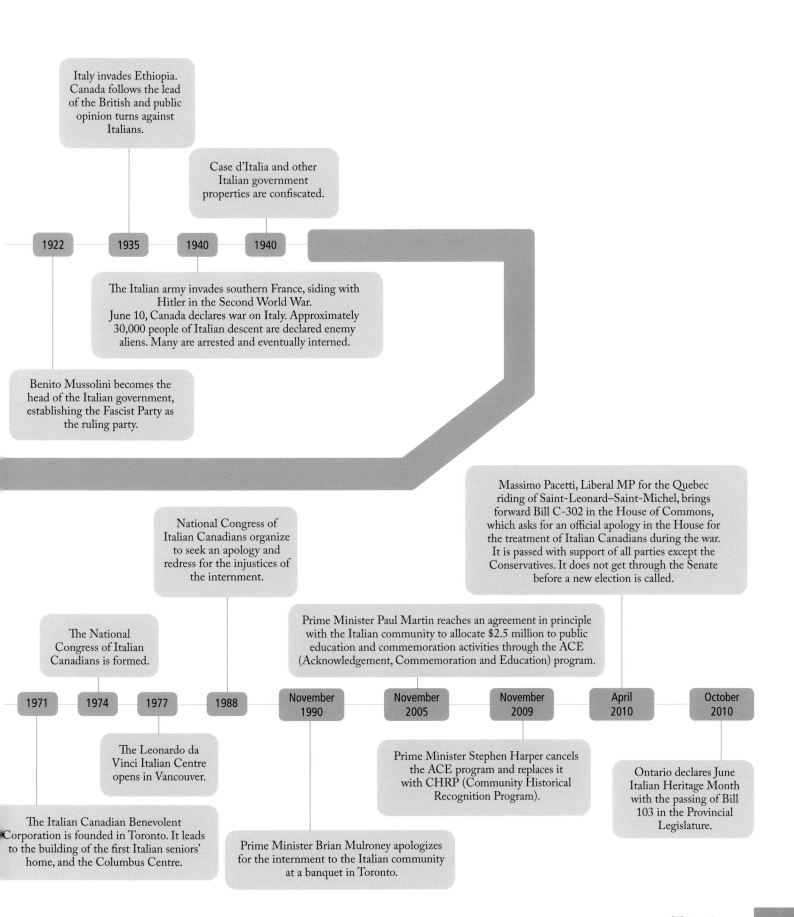

Italy invades Ethiopia. Canada follows the lead of the British and public opinion turns against Italians.

Case d'Italia and other Italian government properties are confiscated.

1922   1935   1940   1940

The Italian army invades southern France, siding with Hitler in the Second World War.
June 10, Canada declares war on Italy. Approximately 30,000 people of Italian descent are declared enemy aliens. Many are arrested and eventually interned.

Benito Mussolini becomes the head of the Italian government, establishing the Fascist Party as the ruling party.

Massimo Pacetti, Liberal MP for the Quebec riding of Saint-Leonard–Saint-Michel, brings forward Bill C-302 in the House of Commons, which asks for an official apology in the House for the treatment of Italian Canadians during the war. It is passed with support of all parties except the Conservatives. It does not get through the Senate before a new election is called.

National Congress of Italian Canadians organize to seek an apology and redress for the injustices of the internment.

Prime Minister Paul Martin reaches an agreement in principle with the Italian community to allocate $2.5 million to public education and commemoration activities through the ACE (Acknowledgement, Commemoration and Education) program.

The National Congress of Italian Canadians is formed.

1971   1974   1977   1988   November 1990   November 2005   November 2009   April 2010   October 2010

The Leonardo da Vinci Italian Centre opens in Vancouver.

Prime Minister Stephen Harper cancels the ACE program and replaces it with CHRP (Community Historical Recognition Program).

Ontario declares June Italian Heritage Month with the passing of Bill 103 in the Provincial Legislature.

The Italian Canadian Benevolent Corporation is founded in Toronto. It leads to the building of the first Italian seniors' home, and the Columbus Centre.

Prime Minister Brian Mulroney apologizes for the internment to the Italian community at a banquet in Toronto.

Glossary

Anglicized: Some members of the Italian community changed their names from Italian-sounding to English-sounding names. For example, Maria Blanco may have become Mary White.

anti-Semitism: Hatred of, or discrimination against, individuals because of their Jewish heritage.

assimilation: The culture of a minority or immigrant group becomes lost within another, more dominant, culture.

bias: A preference or tendency to think or act in a certain way, could be positive or negative.

Casa D'Italia: This was an Italian social and political community centre. A number of fascist clubs, including the Dopolavoro, Gioventù Italiana del Littorio Estero, and the local fascio, were run out of the centre. Case D'Italia is the plural form.

censors: People whose job it is to get rid of material, often written or broadcast, that is considered politically or morally unacceptable. For example, letters written by Italian-Canadian internees were opened and read, and in many cases pieces were blacked out or cut out.

chain migration: When an individual or family immigrated to Canada, often other members of their village or extended family members would follow them.

citizenship: The country that a person belongs to. When you are a citizen of a country, you can have a passport from the country and receive all the rights and benefits that the country offers.

civil rights: The basic privileges that come with being a member of society in a certain country. The right to vote, have an education, and receive justice in the courts are all civil rights.

compensation: The payment of money to make up for a wrong that was done to a person or group.

communism: A political movement that aims to create an equal social order based on common ownership and distribution of material wealth based on need where everyone works for the common good.

conscription: A Canadian government policy that required all able-bodied men eighteen years of age and older to join the military to fight in the war.

curfew: A police or military rule that requires people to keep off the streets during a specific time, often sunset to sunrise.

discrimination: Unjust actions that are caused by a particular mindset or prejudice.; a means of treating people negatively because of their group identity. Discrimination may be based on age, ancestry, gender, language, race, religion, political beliefs, sexual orientation, family status, physical or mental disabilities, appearance, or economic status. Acts of discrimination hurt, humiliate, and isolate the victim.

dispossession: The taking away of a person's belongings, which can include homes, businesses, and personal property.

Dopolavoro: An Italian after-work social club.

emigration: Leaving one's home country to go to a different country.

enemy alien: A person of foreign descent living in a country that is at war with his country of ancestry. A term used in government notices and in the media to describe some Italian Canadians as enemies of the state. The term was applied to Italian citizens eighteen years of age and older as well as those who had received Canadian citizenship since 1922. No proof of crimes against Canada was necessary.

fascism: A political movement that believes in absolute control of a nation under a single authority, or dictator. It does not allow for any opposition and will use violence to crush it. The Fascist party took power in Italy in 1922 and ended its reign in 1943. Amongst other things, Fascism promotes the hatred of Jews, the belief in a superior national race, and total service to the nation by all.

immigration: The arrival of people into a country from their homeland.

impounded: The seizure of a possession from an individual or group by the authorities, such as the police or military. Some Casa d'Italia buildings, documents, and possessions were seized by the government. In other cases, private businesses and personal possessions belonging to Italian Canadians were impounded.

incarceration: Holding someone against his or her will in a guarded place, such as a jail or prison camp.

informant: A person who provides information about certain individuals to authorities, such as the police. The information may cast suspicion on the individuals and get them on a "watch list" or even arrested.

injustice: A wrongful action taken against an individual or group that denies them of their basic rights.

in trust: To place something in the care of someone for safekeeping. All property belonging to Italian Canadians that was impounded by the government was given "in trust" to the Custodian of Enemy Alien Property for safekeeping. In some cases the property was not looked after and lost its value, or it was not returned.

internment: The confinement of people labelled enemies of the state during wartime. Hundreds of men and teenaged boys of Italian ancestry were forced to leave their homes and were sent to remote internment camps in British Columbia, Ontario, or New Brunswick for periods of months to years during the Second World War.

internment camp: The place where hundreds of men of Italian ancestry who were labelled enemy aliens were sent during the war. There were three main internment camps for Italian Canadians: Kananaskis, Petawawa, and Ripples.

left wing: In politics, associated with socialism and Communism.

Mussolini: The leader of the Italian government from December 1922 to July 1943. He was the head of the National Fascist Party and was one of the founders of Italian Fascism. He made many economic improvements in Italy during the 1920s and 1930s and encouraged the spread of Fascism throughout the world to wherever Italians had immigrated, including Canada. As the extreme racist and anti-Semitic views of the party emerged, many Italians abandoned Fascism. Benito Mussolini led Italy to war against Canada and the Allies in 1940. In 1945, following Italy's surrender to the Allies, Mussolini was killed by Italian anti-Fascists in Italy.

navvies: A term used for labourers who worked on construction or excavation projects such as railways and canals.

oppression: Occurs when the feelings, ideas, or demands of an individual or group of people are not recognized or allowed to be expressed by authorities such as the government, justice system, police, or military.

organized crime: Often associated with the Mafia, it refers to groups of individuals who profit from criminal activities such as smuggling, selling illegal drugs, prostitution, and gambling.

padrone: An individual who acted as an employment agent to bring immigrants from Italy to Canada to work. They were usually paid by the immigrant as well as the eventual employer in Canada.

prejudice: An attitude, usually negative, directed toward a person or group of people based on wrong or distorted information. Prejudiced thinking may result in acts of discrimination.

prison camp: A place where individuals were sent to be guarded by the military during the war. Prisoners of war (POWs) were usually citizens of a country that Canada was at war with, or they were individuals who were thought to be a threat to Canada.

propaganda: The spread of specific information, ideas, or images (such as the war posters) to control public opinion or actions.

racism: A belief that one race is superior to another. People are not treated as equals because of their cultural or ethnic differences. Racism may be systemic (part of institutions, governments, organizations, and programs) or part of the attitudes and behaviour of individuals.

redress: To right a wrong, sometimes by

compensating the victim or by punishing the wrongdoer. Refers to the movement within the Italian-Canadian community for an official apology and payment for the injustices of the government's actions toward Italian-Canadians during the Second World War.

registration: A person is required to report to an authority and give his or her name, place of residence, and other personal information and it is kept on record.

right wing: In politics, the extreme right is associated with fascism, nazism, and other non-democratic movements.

social assistance: Money provided by the government to help out those who are in poverty.

sympathizer: A person who is thought to be in favour of a particular group, policy, or idea.

textile: Fabric.

totalitarian: A type of political system in which one person has absolute control and dictates what everyone else must do. There are no elections for the one in charge. No opposition to the leader is permitted.

War Measures Act: A Canadian law that gave the government the right to label individuals as enemy aliens and take away their civil rights, such as the right to be presumed innocent.

For Further Reading

Non-Fiction Books:

Bowen, Lynne. *Whoever Gives Us Bread: The Story of Italians in British Columbia*. Vancouver, BC: Douglas & McIntyre, 2011.

Carbone, Stanislao. *Italians in Winnipeg: An Illustrated History*. Winnipeg, MB: University of Manitoba Press, 1998.

Culos, Raymond. *Injustice Served. The story of British Columbia's Italian Enemy Aliens during World War II.* Montreal: Cusmano Books, 2012.

Della Valle, Madelyn, ed. *Impronte: Italian Imprints in Windsor*. Windsor, ON: Walkerville Publishing, 2009.

Di Sciascio-Andrews, Josie. *How the Italians Created Canada: From Giovanni Caboto to the Cultural Renaissance*. Edmonton, AB: Dragon Hill Publishing, 2008.

Iacovetta, Franca, Roberto Perin, and Angelo Principe, eds. *Enemies Within: Italian and Other Internees in Canada and Abroad*. Toronto: University of Toronto Press, 2000.

Il Postino (series). *Memories to Memorial: The Internment of Ottawa's Italian Canadians during the Second World War*. Ottawa: Preston Street Community Foundation, 2011.

Migliore, Sam, and A. Evo DiPierro. *Italian Lives, Cape Breton Memories*. Sydney, NS: Cape Breton University Press, 1999.

Perin, Roberto, and Franc Sturino, eds. *Arrangiarsi: The Italian Immigration Experience in Canada*. Toronto: Guernica Editions, 2006.

Pietropaolo, Vincenzo. *Not Paved with Gold: Italian-Canadian Immigrants in the 1970s*. Toronto: Between the Lines, 2006.

Ramirez, Bruno. *The Italians in Canada*. Ottawa: Canadian Historical Association, 1989.

Films/Audio Recordings:

Little Italies, 6 CD set. "A journey into the drama of growing up Italian in Canada." CBC Audio. ISBN: 0660195844

Barbed Wire and Mandolins. Film by Nicola Zavaglia, 1997, 48 minutes. This is a short documentary introducing Italian Canadians whose lives were disrupted when they were interned during the Second World War. It can be viewed online at the National Film Board's website (www.nfb.ca).

Piazza Petawawa
http://www.icff.ca/piazza-petawawa/
This is a 28 minute Canadian documentary directed by Rino Noto on the internment, produced in 2012.

The Italian Question
http://www.italianquestion.com/main.html
The Italian Question is a new documentary film and website project on the internment of Italian Canadians at the outbreak of the Second World War. It was produced by Aysha Productions Inc., commissioned by York University, and funded by the Government of Canada through the Community Historical Recognition Program.

Websites:

www.canadese.org – This is the website for the National Congress of Italian Canadians, Toronto. There are many other branches of the NCIC and they have their own websites.

www.nbinternmentcampmuseum.ca – This website tells the story of the internment camp Ripples, in Minto, New Brunswick.

www.italianculturalcentre.ca – This is the website for the Italian Cultural Centre in Vancouver, British Columbia. In March 2012 they launched an exhibit entitled "Beyond the Barbed Wire: Experiences of Italian Canadians in WW2," along with additional materials relating to the subject.

www.civilisations.ca/cmc/exhibitions/cultur/presenza/pszase. shtml – The Virtual Museum of Canada has a good exhibit called "Presenza: A New look at Italian-Canadian Heritage," which includes the history of Italian immigration to Canada.

www.cic.gc.ca/english/multiculturalism/programs/community-projects.asp#it – This site offers a list of projects funded by the CHRP program to educate the public about the Italian-Canadian internment.

www.italiancanadianww2.ca/ - This is the website for the Columbus Centre, Toronto. Their project, Italian Canadians as Enemy Aliens: Memories of World War II is an excellent source of information and first person live video interviews, some of which are linked in this book.

WATCH THE VIDEO

Look for this symbol throughout the book for links to video clips available on the website *Italian Canadians as Enemy Aliens: Memories of World War II*, at www.italiancanadianww2.ca

Accenti Issue 23, Fall 2011: p. 98 (top right)

Angela Hickman: p. 40 (right), 41 (bottom left), 96 (top), 103 (left)

Archives of Manitoba: p. 5 (centre left), 17 (bottom), 44 (left, SIS N19973)

Archives of Ontario: p. 14 (top, I0048256), 17 (top, D2004-18532), 22 (left, I0016160; right, I0011593), 31 (middle left, I0048255), 46 (top, I0041103), 94 (right, I0048258), 75 (top, I0041100; bottom, I0041101)

Arnold Iannuzzi, private collection: p. 60, 82, 92

Bagnell, Kenneth. *Canadese: A Portrait of the Italian Canadians.* Toronto: Macmillan of Canada, 1989. p. 19 (bottom right), 20 (bottom), 21 (bottom), 27 (top), 29 (bottom right), 61 (top), 85 (right), 98 (bottom left)

Barzini, Luigi Giorgio. *The Italians.* New York: Atheneum, 1964. p. 9 (top right), 48 (left)

The Beaton Institute, Cape Breton University: p. 24, 86 (bottom), 69 (top)

Benny Ferri, private collection: p. 89 (bottom), 90 (right)

Canadian Labour Congress: p. 99 (bottom right)

Canadian Museum of Civilization: p. 18 (D2004-6137), 20 (top, D2004-6149), 29 (top right, D2004-6144), 33 (top, ITA-200152)

Canadian Museum of Immigration at Pier 21: p. 95 (all)

Canadian War Museum: p. 52 (left, 19750251-008), 54 (right, 19750317-052), 55 (bottom left, 19750317-048)

Carbone, Stanislao. *Italians in Winnipeg: An Illustrated History.* Winnipeg: University of Manitoba Press, 1998. p. 14 (bottom), 15 (all), 16 (bottom left & right), 19 (bottom left), 28 (all), 30 (bottom), 41 (top), 42 (top right), 43 (middle & bottom), 45 (bottom), 54 (left), 55 (top left)

————. *The Streets Were Not Paved with Gold: A Social History of Italians in Winnipeg.* Winnipeg: Manitoba Italian Heritage Committee, 1993. p. 39 (bottom), 96 (bottom)

Careless, J. M. S. *Toronto to 1918: An Illustrated History.* Toronto: James Lorimer & Company Ltd., 1984. p. 23 (top), 30 (top)

Chilliwack Museum and Archives: p. 5 (top)

City of Toronto Archives: p. 5 (bottom right, Fonds 1244, Item 8143), 26 (top, Series 376, File 4, Item 21; bottom, Series 372, Sub-Series 59, Item 42), 33 (bottom), 35 (bottom), 38 (bottom) 39 (top, Series 372, Sub-Series 32, Item 404), 40 (left, Fonds 1244, Item 8143), 45 (middle, Fonds 1244, Item 1945), 52 (right, Series 340, Subseries 8, File 73), 53 (top, Fonds F1266, Item 68266), 55 (top right, Fonds 1266, Item 65864; bottom right, Fonds 1266, item 75876), 58 (top, f1266_it66758; middle, f1266_it66761; bottom, f1266_it66766), 59 (bottom right, f1266_it66763), 64 (bottom, f1266_it66768), 85 (left, Fonds 1266, Item 20662)

Columbus Centre of Toronto: p. 59 (bottom left), 68

Connie Hickman: p. 36 (bottom), 97 (bottom), 103 (bottom right)

De Luna, Giovanni et al. *L'Italia del Novecento, Le fotografie e la storia, Il potere da Giolitti a Mussolini (1900-1945).* Turin: G. Einaudi, 2005. p. 11 (middle & bottom), 12 (right), 13 (top)

Della Valle, Madelyn, ed. *Impronte: Italian Imprints in Windsor.* Windsor: Walkerville Publishing, 2009: p. 7, 31 (bottom), 34 (top left & right), 97 (top left), 70 (all), 71 (top)

Eleanor Mogavero Loreti, private collection: p. 41 (bottom right), 89 (top), 67

Elson, Robert T. *Prelude to War: World War II.* Chicago: Time-Life Books, 1977: p. 6, 49 (bottom)

Enrica Pataracchia Violin, private collection: p. 78 (all), 79 (top), 81 (bottom)

Esposito, Phil, and Tony Esposito, with Tim Moriarty. *The Brothers Esposito.* New York: Hawthorn Books, 1971. p. 98 (top left)

Family of Leonardo Frenza via Columbus Centre of Toronto: p. 93 (top)

Filoso, Angelo, Ariella Dal Farra Hostetter, and Francesca L'Orfano. *Memories to Memorial: The Internment of Ottawa's Italian Canadians during the Second World War.* Ottawa: Italian Canadian Community Centre of the National Capital Region, 2011. p. 81 (top), 83 (all), 84 (top), 91 (middle), 93 (bottom)

Gendel, Milton. *An Illustrated History of Italy.* New York: McGraw-Hill, 1966. p. 13 (bottom)

George Iantorno, private collection: p. 65 (top, middle)

Giuliano, Bruce B. *Sacro O Profano?: A Consideration of Four Italian-Canadian Religious Festivals.* Ottawa: National Museums of Canada, 1976. p. 37 (bottom), 42 (top left)

Hamilton Public Library: p. 25 (top)

The Hamilton Spectator: p. 63

Harney, Robert F., and Harold Troper. *Immigrants: A Portrait of the Urban Experience, 1890–1930.* Toronto: Van Nostrand Reinhold, 1975. p. 19 (top right)

The Hon. Frank Iacobucci and the Frank Iacobucci Centre for Italian Canadian Studies: p. 99 (top left)

Iacovetta, Franca, Roberto Perin, and Angelo Principe, eds. *Enemies Within: Italian and Other Internees in Canada and Abroad.* Toronto: University of Toronto Press, 2000. p. 46 (bottom), 48 (right), 101 (bottom left)

Il Postino Vol. 12, No. 10, July 2011: p. 99 (bottom left)

Jean Smith Cavalluzzo, private collection: 49 (top right), 80, 90 (left), 103 (middle)

John Edward de Toro via Columbus Centre of Toronto: p. 81 (middle)

Jucker, Ninetta. *Italy.* London: Thames & Hudson, 1970. p. 9 (top left)

Keith Minchin, Faces of Fredericton: p. 69 (bottom), 71 (bottom left), 72 (all), 73 (all), 74 (all), 76 (bottom), 102

Library and Archives Canada: p. 19 (top left, PA-025448), 21 (top, C-30620), 29 (bottom left, PA-091104), 31 (top right, PA-091122), 45 (top left; top right, 2837956), 53 (bottom, e006079006), 56 (PA-161458), 62 (right, PA-211002)

Lorenzetti family, private collection: p. 35 (top left)

Lorimer, James. *The Ex: A Picture History of the Canadian National Exhibition.* James Lewis & Samuel, 1973. p. 23 (left)

Martinello family, private collection: p. 37 (middle), 87

Martino, Arcangelo. *Italian Roots and Canadian Blossoms: A History of Brantford's Italian-Canadian Community 1880–1999.* Brantford, ON: Almar Publishing, 2000. p. 11 (top), 35 (top right)

Massimo Pacetti, private collection: p. 101 (bottom right)

Mazzadi, Luisa. *L'Italia umbertina: immagini di un'epoca.* Milan: Rusconi, 1982. p. 8 (left), 9 (middle & bottom), 10 (all)

Metropolitan Toronto Library Board: p. 42 (bottom)

Migliore, Sam, and A. Evo DiPierro. *Italian Lives, Cape Breton Memories.* Sydney, NS: University College of Cape Breton Press, 1999. p. 62 (left), 79 (bottom), 91 (bottom)

Miller, Carman. *Canada's Little War: Fighting for the British Empire in Southern Africa 1899–1902.* Toronto: James Lorimer & Company Ltd., 1973. p. 23 (right)

Multicultural History Society of Ontario: p. 25 (bottom, ITA-200334), 32 (left, ITA-200152), 32 (right), 34 (bottom, ITA-200102), 36 (top, ITA-40), 43 (top, ITA-14), 44 (right), 50 (left), 94 (left, ITA-100323)

Nadeau, Jean-François. *The Canadian Fuhrer: The Life of Adrien Arcand.* Trans. Bob Chodos, Eric Hamovich, and Susan Joanis. Toronto: James Lorimer & Company Ltd., 2011. p. 51 (all)

New Brunswick Internment Camp Museum: p. 76–77 (top)

Nicaso, Antonio. *Rocco Perri: The Story of Canada's Most Notorious Bootlegger.* Toronto: John Wiley & Sons, 2004. p. 29 (top left)

Nino Ricci, private collection: p. 99 (top right)

Norwich, John Julius, ed. *The Italians: History, Art and the Genius of a People.* New York: Harry N. Abrams, 1983. p. 8 (right), 12 (left)

Principe, Angelo. *The Darkest Side of the Fascist Years.* Toronto: Guernica, 1999. p. 47 (middle & bottom), 49 (top left)

Ramírez, Bruno. *Les premiers Italiens de Montréal: L'origine de la Petite Italie du Québec.* Montreal: Boréal Express, 1984. p. 16 (top), 27 (bottom), 37 (top)

Roberto Portolese, via Columbus Centre of Toronto: p. 97 (top right)

Ronald Caplan, *Cape Breton's Magazine*: p. 88

Rose Papalia Santagato, private collection: p. 31 (top left), 47 (top), 65 (bottom), 86 (top)

Toronto Star Archives / GetStock.com: p. 57 (top)

United Church of Canada Archives: p. 38 (top)

Who's Who in Canada, 1930–31. Toronto: International Press, 1931. p. 91 (top)

Windsor's Community Museum: p. 66 (all)

Windsor Star: p. 57 (bottom), 59 (top), 64 (top)

The Young Worker: p. 50 (right)

Zaffiro family, private collection: p. 61 (bottom), 84 (bottom)

Zucchi, John E. *Italians in Toronto: Development of a National Identity 1875–1935.* Kingston and Montreal: McGill-Queens University Press, 1988. p. 25 (middle), 27 (middle)

Index